Beyond
Customer Satisfaction
to
Customer Loyalty

The Key to Greater Profitability

Keki R. Bhote

AMA Management Briefing

AMA MEMBERSHIP PUBLICATIONS DIVISION
AMERICAN MANAGEMENT ASSOCIATION

For information on how to order additional copies of this publication, see page 151

Library of Congress Cataloging-in-Publication Data

Bhote, Keki R., 1925–
    Beyond customer satisfaction to customer loyalty : the key to greater profitability / Keki R. Bhote.
        p. cm.—(AMA management briefing)
    Includes bibliographical references.
    ISBN 0-8144-2362-0
    1. Consumer satisfaciton. 2. Customer services. 3. Customer relations. I. Title. II. Series.
HF5415.5.B486 1996
658.8'12—dc20   96-35335
                                    CIP

10 9 8 7 6 5 4 3 2 1

The Old Testament

- Customer Satisfaction
- Quality (for its own sake)
- Cost Reduction
- Market Share
- Market Research

The New Testament

- Customer Loyalty
- Customer Retention
- Zero Defections
- Lifelong Customers

The main objective of a supplier is to create and nurture satisfied, repetitive and loyal customers who have received—and perceived that they have received—*added value* from the supplier. . . . Keki R. Bhote

Contents

Introduction

"You may think that you make products, but you really make loyal customers. You may think that you make sales, but you really make loyal customers."

—Mark Hanan & Peter Karp

THE NEED FOR THIS BRIEFING

Chairman Pat Connors was reviewing the year-end customer satisfaction measurements of his company, Electro-Dynamics, with his staff. Like many companies, Electro-Dynamics periodically surveyed a random sample of customers to determine their overall satisfaction with the company's products and services. The customers rated the company using a standard five-point scale, with 1 indicating "very dissatisfied," and 5 "very satisfied."

Electro-Dynamics' customers indicated they were generally pleased with the company's performance, as shown in FIGURE 1.

Connors asked his senior executives what they thought about the scorecard. There was general agreement that Electro-Dynamics was in good standing with its customers. Indeed, the overall ratings were moving up. The company had been measuring the ratio of the "satisfied" and "very satisfied" added together and divided by the "very dissatisfied" and "dissatisfied" added together. The ratio was nearly 6:1, an improvement over the previous survey of 4.6:1.

After the staff had finished patting themselves on the back, Pat threw a bombshell into their midst.

"Gentlemen," he said, "I commissioned a follow-up survey that

FIGURE 1: Customer Satisfaction Survey Results

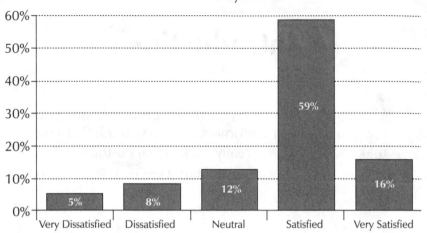

asked the same customers, 'Would you return to us the next time you need our product?' Among the 'very satisfied' group, 98% answered yes. But among the 'satisfied' group, only 70% said they would return. Gentlemen, we are faced with a defection rate of about 20%, even disregarding the 'neutral,' 'dissatisfied,' and 'very dissatisfied' responses. This is no time to feel smug; we have a full-blown crisis on our hands!"

Electro-Dynamics is a hypothetical company and Pat Connors a fictitious CEO. But the lessons drawn from this example are very real and very frightening to companies that focus merely on customer satisfaction as a measure of business performance.

"It's Customer Loyalty, Stupid"

During the 1992 election campaign, the Clinton slogan was "It's the economy, stupid." The economy was uppermost in the minds of American voters, and it was simply not enough to concentrate on soft issues like family values. Similarly, we can now say that it is no longer enough to concentrate on customer satisfaction—the slogan of so many well-meaning companies—but to graduate to *customer loyalty*. To paraphrase an expression in mathematics, customer satisfaction is a necessary but by no means a sufficient condition for an enterprise. Dr. W.

Edwards Deming, the renowned quality guru, put it succinctly: "A merely satisfied customer will go elsewhere when a competitor cuts its prices!"

The Juran Institute Survey

A study by the prestigious Juran Institute, founded by another quality guru, Dr. Joseph M. Juran, reinforces this point. The survey of 200 of the largest companies in the United States found:

- A full 90% of the top managers of these companies were convinced that "maximizing customer satisfaction maximizes profitability and market share."
- However, fewer than 30% were confident that economic value had been added as a result of their customer satisfaction efforts.
- And *fewer than* 2% were able to measure a bottom-line improvement resulting from documented increases in levels of customer satisfaction!

These startling results fly in the face of conventional wisdom, which asserts that if you ensure customer satisfaction, profits will take care of themselves.

The Objective of This Briefing

The purpose of this briefing is to detail:

- a clear picture of why customer satisfaction—the new buzzword—in so-called enlightened companies is inadequate for achieving a truly competitive advantage.
- the importance of graduating from mere customer satisfaction to customer loyalty, zero customer defection, and lifelong customer retention.
- the four stages in the evolution of customer loyalty—from the innocent stage to world class stage.
- the differences among various groups of customers and the need to concentrate on "core" customers, who constitute fewer than

20% of a company's total customers but command over 80% of the sales dollars.

- the inviolate principles of customer loyalty to which most companies pay scant attention, but which can be ignored only at their peril.
- a seven-step roadmap to attain and maintain customer loyalty.
- an audit by which a company can assess its customer loyalty effectiveness at each step of the roadmap.

The Benefits of This Briefing

Concentrating on the methods described in this briefing will enable a company to

- not only reduce the defection rate of its customers, but actually *increase* their retention rate.
- convert one-time customers into lifelong customers, not only for a specific product or service, but for the whole portfolio of a company's offerings.
- achieve a breakthrough profit improvement—50% and more—by concentrating on customer loyalty, rather than run-of-the-mill approaches such as cost reduction or market share enhancement.
- make employee empowerment real, instead of just another non-productive fad or slogan.

Part I of the briefing opens by defining four stages in a company's evolution toward building customer loyalty. In my prior publications, I developed similar four-stage models of evolution for quality, supply management, cost, and cycle time. This model is the latest in the series. Part I continues by presenting a compelling case for customer loyalty as the sine qua non of growth and profitability and summarizes the key management principles that must guide the transition. Part II provides a seven-step roadmap and audit to guide the company in this new direction.

Part 1

Transition from Customer Satisfaction to Customer Loyalty

1

The Four Stages in the Evolution of Customer Loyalty

"How robust is your company's customer health?"

—Keki R. Bhote

From Customer Innocence to Customer Heaven

In the last two decades, industry has progressed from a relatively elementary stage to world class in several fields—quality, design manufacturing, cycle time, supply management, and the like. This chapter outlines a similar progression in a company's perspective on its customers—from a primitive Stage 1 to a world class Stage 4.

A company in Stage 1, called the Innocent Stage, is in the Dark Ages of customer consciousness. A company in Stage 2, called the Awakened Stage, recognizes the importance of the customer but thrashes around without a firm game plan. A company in Stage 3, called the Progressive Stage, has established an infrastructure for customer satisfaction. A company in Stage 4, called the World Class Stage, has earned maximum customer loyalty and has entered the kingdom of customer heaven.

TABLE 1 shows the four stages in the evolution of customer loyalty on one leg of the matrix and 10 customer-related characteristics within a company on the other leg. These characteristics are scope, focus, customer segmentation, management, organization, goals, cus-

TABLE 1: The Four Stages in the Evolution of Customer Loyalty

Characteristic	Stage 1: Innocent	Stage 2: Awakened	Stage 3: Progressive	Stage 4: World Class
1. Scope	Inward preoccupation	Cost reduction driven	Competition driven	Adding value to customer
2. Focus	Commodity	Technology/quality	Customer satisfaction	Customer loyalty
3. Customer segmentation	No differentiation	Elimination of "dog" customers	Internal customer and company stakeholders	Core customers
4. Management	Bureaucratic, dictatorial	Micro-management	Coach	Vision, inspiration, leadership
5. Organization	Vertical management	Matrix management	Delayering; flat pyramid	Cross-functional teams; CCO
6. Goals	Fighting "forest fires"	Making the budget	Meeting customer expectations	Delighting customers
7. Customer Requirements	Determined by management/engineering	Determined by market research	Determined by conjoint analysis, other techniques	Determined by QFD
8. Customer Measurements	Maximize sales, profits	Minimize complaints	Maximize market share	Maximize customer retention
9. Analysis of Feedback	Little or no follow-up	Survey instruments never changed	Customer satisfaction index (CSI)	Former and noncustomers analyzed
10. Improvement Tools	Seven tools of QC	Brainstorming and statistical tools	Creative tools: VE and force field analysis	Business process reengineering

tomer requirements, customer measurements, analysis of customer feedback, and improvement tools.

The table can be likened to a company's "customer health chart." Stage 1 companies are terminally ill. Stage 2 companies need hospitalization. Stage 3 companies require periodic checkups. Stage 4 companies enjoy robust health. TABLE 1 is simple to apply and can be evaluated either by the company's own management or by its core customers. Let's take a closer look at the customer-related characteristics associated with each of the four stages.

1. Scope: From Self-Centered to Adding Value to the Customer

In the primitive Stage 1, a company is inward looking and obsessed with internal priorities. It considers the customer incidental, at best, and as a pest, at worst.

In Stage 2, a company mounts a concerted drive for cost reduction as the way to attract customers, who—in its view—would otherwise go to its competition. Many companies still languish in Stage 2.

In Stage 3, a company intensifies its battle against competition by offering features to match the competition's, regardless of whether the features are important or not to its customers. It is saddled with "feature creep"!

In Stage 4, a company truly believes that its main objective is to add value to its core customers (those 20% or less of total customers who account for 80% or more of total sales). Value translates to quality, cost, cycle time, technology, and other benefits that the customers perceive they receive, and that they cannot achieve by themselves. A company in Stage 4 is truly world class.

2. Focus: From Commodity Focus to Customer Loyalty

In Stage 1, a company's products and services are essentially the same as those offered by competitors. It is in the commodity business, focusing on price and volume. Stage 1 is characteristic of many companies in the first half of the 20th century.

In Stage 2, a company uses technology to stay ahead of competition and gain a quasi-monopoly position. But it requires massive investments in R&D, numerous production changes, and costly field fixes. In today's "global village," when communications and technology travel from country to country at the speed of light, these advantages are temporary. Yet many companies in the West cling to technology as the silver bullet of competitive advantage.

Stage 2 is also characteristic of companies with a quality focus.

They regard quality as the Shangri-la of the business world. But it is worshipped for its own sake, not for what it can do for customers. The emphasis is on internal parameters, such as defect reduction, conformance to engineering requirements, and cost reduction. The latest fad is total quality management (TQM). Stage 2 companies spend millions of dollars on it, yet have no appreciable improvement in either customer satisfaction or in the southeast corner of the P&L statement. Stage 2 is characteristic of at least 50% of companies—even today.

In Stage 3, the focus shifts to customer satisfaction. Price, technology, and quality are only prerequisites. They are not sufficient to differentiate a company's products or services from those of the competitors. Customer satisfaction means listening to customer requirements first and then ensuring that those requirements are delivered to achieve full customer satisfaction. Even in the 1990s, however, fewer than one-third of all companies have a comprehensive customer satisfaction focus. The reasons for this are detailed in Chapter 3.

In Stage 4, world class companies go well beyond customer satisfaction; they strive for and achieve zero customer defection. They delight customers and earn their loyalty—often for life. How to reach this stage is the objective of this entire briefing.

3. Customer Segmentation:
From Nondiscrimination to Core Customers

In Stage 1, there is little or no differentiation among the various types of customers. They are treated alike, generally without much attention to any single customer or groups of customers.

In Stage 2, the "dog" customers—those that are not worth keeping for reasons of low profitability, low future potential, dishonesty, or just plain nuisance—are candidates for elimination.

In Stage 3, a company expands its horizons to include internal customers—a group that is almost as important as external customers. It also looks upon its other stakeholders—especially its distributors, dealers, suppliers, and its employees—as "customers" that need tender loving care.

In Stage 4, all the resources of a company are marshaled to serve core customers. Their defection would warrant pushing the company's panic button. Their retention and their loyalty become an obsession.

4. Management: From Boss to Coach; From Manager to Leader

It is an axiom that everything starts and ends with top management. This is as true for customers as it is for quality, design, manufacturing, supply management, and other major activities of a company.

In Stage 1, management looks upon customers as incidental, at best, and as a nuisance, at worst. Its management style is bureaucratic and dictatorial. It rules by fear and intimidation. Customer-contact employees—those frontline troops that come into daily contact with the customer—are picked off the street, given little or no training, and treated as pairs of hands.

In Stage 2, managers grudgingly acknowledge the customer's importance. But they formulate rules for their own convenience, rather than for their importance or benefit to customers. These rules are rigidly enforced by a command-and-control management that has little trust for its employees and makes all the decisions in the style known as micromanagement.

In Stage 3, the customer's importance is appreciated and accelerated. Rules for the convenience of management still exist, but they can be bent to suit the larger interest of customers. Managers begin to shed their bossy style and move toward the role of coach and mentor.

In Stage 4, the customer is *king* and core customers are worshipped. Rules for the convenience of management are jettisoned and all actions are determined by whether they advance the interests of customers. Managers are transformed into leaders, providing vision and inspiration to their employees, trusting them, supporting them, and helping them reach their maximum potential. Unfortunately, over 95% of CEOs are managers; fewer than 5% are true leaders!

5. Organization: From Vertical Silos to Cross-Functional Teams

In Stage 1, a company employs a bureaucratic pattern of vertical management, where communications tend to flow up and down, from and to the boss. But customers and problems don't always respect the organizational chart: They tend to move horizontally. Stage 1 promotes a vertical "silo" mentality, where high departmental walls tend to protect "turfs."

In Stage 2, matrix management, under a product manager or project leader, proves to be more suited to serve customers than the Stage 1 vertical organization. On the other hand, the matrix structure, with two "bosses," can be confusing and disruptive.

In Stage 3, the tall pyramid with multiple layers of managers between the CEO and the worker is delayered, yielding to a flat pyramid with no more than four or five such levels between the CEO and the worker. The result is that a manager, with 50 people to manage rather than 6 to 10, can no longer micromanage. His people must be allowed the freedom to fulfill the company's goals and their own goals, with the manager providing guidance and coaching, rather than commanding and controlling. The employees' sights are better focused on customers, with less energy wasted on internal preoccupations. Sadly, micromanagement is still the order of the day in most companies.

In Stage 4, the team concept makes the organization chart quasi-obsolete. Cross-functional teams are formed—their preeminent goal to serve customers. The company appoints a senior executive as a CCO (chief customer officer), with a status second only to the CEO. Such a CCO has the power to marshal the total resources of the company to achieve customer loyalty.

6. Goals: From Fighting Customer Fires to Delighting Customers

In Stage 1, a company is in a reactive mode, responding to "forest fires" at the point when the fires begin to burn out of control. Goals and key decisions are arbitrary, subjective, and susceptible to the changing whims of an entrepreneurial owner/CEO.

In Stage 2, a company's goal is making the budget. It has tight financial controls structured around a comprehensive budgeting and control process. Budget results are more important than fulfilling customer expectations or confronting competition. Stage 2 is, regrettably, the state of affairs in most companies.

In Stage 3, a company's goal is to meet and exceed customer expectations. It utilizes nonfinancial performance measures to drive management decisions and does not rely merely on budget performance. It has long-term goals and planning horizons of one to five years, rather than a slavish acquiescence to the tyranny of financial analysts with their quarter-by-quarter demands.

In Stage 4, a company goes beyond its goals of simple customer satisfaction to customer delight, customer enthusiasm, customer excitement, customer "wow." It reaches for features and services that customers have not expected or anticipated but which thrill them and raise their LQ (loyalty quotient).

7. Customer Requirements:
From "Voice of Management" to "Voice of the Customer"

In Stage 1, a company's management and/or its design group determines the customers' requirements without any input from the customers. They think they know the customers' needs better than the customers themselves! The results: 8 out of 10 new products and services fail in the marketplace.

In Stage 2, market research is used to obtain customer inputs. But market research, as generally practiced, has several shortcomings. It deals more with the demographics of customers rather than with their desires—and it does not have the depth of technical knowledge to probe these desires. Thus, it becomes one more filter between the customer and those people in the company who need firsthand communication with their customers. Sadly, most companies languish in Stage 2.

In Stage 3, a number of imaginative techniques are used to determine customer requirements. They include value research, the windows model, sensitivity analysis, multiattribute evaluation, and conjoint analysis. These techniques, explained in Chapter 8, all put the customer at center stage. However, many companies are not aware of their utility.

In Stage 4, quality function deployment (QFD) is employed. QFD, a technique developed 25 years ago in Japan's Kobe shipyards, is widely used in that country; it is now emerging as the most powerful technique of all in America and, to a lesser extent, in Europe. It determines each important customer requirement, its priority for customers, and how a company stacks up against its best competition for that requirement. Various matrix analyses help the engineers develop a product or service that meets the customers' requirements in ways that will outflank competition. QFD is explained in more detail in Chapter 8. Finally, mass customization, also discussed in Chapter 8, begins to replace mass marketing.

8. Customer Measurements: From Profit to Customer Loyalty

In Stage 1, a company believes that its main objective is profit. But it does not realize that profit is an output, not an input—an effect, not a cause. Management becomes so mesmerized with sales revenues and margins that the company achieves neither customer satisfaction nor adequate profit!

In Stage 2, a company receives customer feedback in only the most elementary manner. It uses warranty figures and complaints or claims as the sole measures of performance for customers.

In Stage 3, a company relies on market share as a customer satisfaction gauge. But market share measures only the quantity of customers, not their satisfaction—and certainly not their loyalty over time. Most companies still rely on market share as a customer gauge. But it can be a tranquilizer, giving a false euphoria and a misleading indication of customer continuity. Then—a few quarters later—the bottom drops out as customers get fed up and defect. A great majority of companies are between Stage 2 and Stage 3.

In Stage 4, a company goes the whole nine yards to measure customer loyalty. It monitors defection rates, entices former customers back to its fold, and researches noncustomers. It concentrates not only on retention of customers but on their longevity.

9. Analysis of Feedback:
From Zero to Probing Former Customers and Noncustomers

In Stage 1, a company does little or no follow-up on the feedback from customer surveys or measurements. Management does not listen to its customer-contact employees' inputs on customers, or does not believe the revealed shortcomings.

In Stage 2, a company continues to administer the same survey instruments to its customers, disregarding changes needed in the instruments because of dynamic changes in the marketplace. It fears that there would be no way to compare customer satisfaction scores if the baseline of questions were changed. To such a company, a score seems more important than the required improvement. Surprisingly, 40% of companies are still mired in Stage 2.

In Stage 3, a company uses a customer satisfaction index (CSI). A

CSI, explained more fully in Chapter 11, combines the most important customer requirements and the company's rating on each requirement to establish a single index, representing the company's scorecard as well as its best competitor's scorecard. In Stage 4, a company extends its horizons beyond its current customers to analyze the reasons former customers have defected, then tries to win them back. The company goes further, analyzing why its noncustomers do not use its products and services but rather those of its competitors.

10. Improvement Tools: From Kindergarten Levels to Ph.D. Levels

In Stage 1, a company is rarely concerned with improving its customer performance. If it uses any improvement tools at all, it employs the seven tools of quality control—these are elementary tools, such as plan-do-study-act (PDSA), Pareto charts, frequency distributions, and control charts. They hardly scratch the surface of meaningful improvement.

In Stage 2, a company employs somewhat more powerful tools, such as brainstorming, cause-and-effect diagrams, and pre-control. This author is also researching the extension of design of experiments (DOE) techniques—so powerful in product problem solving and problem prevention—to the administrative areas of a company, including the customer. These are outlined briefly in Chapter 12. Over 90% of companies are still stuck in Stage 2.

In Stage 3, a company harnesses creative tools like value engineering and force field analysis to explore imaginative ways to improve customer satisfaction and loyalty.

Finally, in Stage 4, a company marshals the latest techniques of business process reengineering (BPR) to flowchart all business processes affecting the customer, eliminating all non-value-added steps, and then—using "out-of-box" thinking—develops revolutionary ways to dramatically improve such processes, in terms of quality, cost, cycle time, and—above all—customer delight.

A Long Way to Go

Even though a company may fall into several of the various stages described in the "customer health chart" (TABLE 1), it is my personal opinion—after consulting with over 350 companies—that the great majority of companies are still mired in Stage 2, with a small distribution tail in Stage 1 and an even tinier distribution tail in Stage 3. As the saying goes, "Baby, you have a long way to go!"

2

Customer Differentiation: Focus on "Core" Customers

"You do not have to satisfy everyone. There are many customers whose satisfaction is irrelevant. But the satisfaction (loyalty) of some customers is so crucial to your success, as well as to your survival, that not only must you satisfy them best; you must satisfy them always."

—Mark Hanan & Peter Karp

The Concentration Decision

Peter Drucker, the management guru par excellence, has stated that a company cannot afford to be in too many businesses at the same time. It must make a decision to concentrate on businesses in which it excels. Tom Peters and Robert Waterman, in their book *In Search of Excellence* (Harper & Row, 1982), emphasize the same concept when they state that companies "should stick to their knitting"—that is, concentrate on those businesses in which they are the most competent.

The BCG Portfolio Analysis

In the early 1980s, many companies began using the Boston Consulting Group's now-famous system of "portfolio analysis" to evaluate the company's competence in each strategic business unit (SBU) vs. the industry attractiveness of the SBU. Although intended for product evaluation, the analysis can also be used to evaluate a company's portfolio of customers.

The traditional analysis divides SBUs into four categories:

1. The "dog" SBUs, with low competency and low industry attractiveness, should be divested.
2. "Cash cow" SBUs, with high competency but low industry attractiveness, should be "milked"; i.e., no resources need be poured in, but they should be pumped to provide cash for the question mark and star SBUs.
3. "Question mark" SBUs, with low competency but high industry attractiveness, should be nurtured with cash inflows from the cash cow SBUs to move them into the star category.
4. "Star" SBUs, with both high competency and high industry attractiveness, should be the company's major focus.

The curved lines in FIGURE 2 approximate product life cycles, as managed by U.S. companies and their more aggressive global competitors. The former tend to keep the "dog" businesses longer because of historic or sentimental reasons. (Often it is one of these businesses that started the company, and its founders or senior management hate to make a divestiture, despite its deterioration to "dog" status.) Another prevalent problem is that U.S. companies do not milk their "cash cow" SBUs to the fullest extent before they degenerate into the "dog" category. U.S. companies also tend to retain their "question mark" businesses much longer than their better global competitors; when these advance to star businesses they tend to remain in that category for too short a time, as compared to their global competitors' star SBUs.

The Customer Portfolio Analysis

FIGURE 3, modeled after the BCG portfolio analysis, provides a technique for differentiating between types of customers. The figure shows two axes, based on the two fundamental objectives of any company: relative company profitability and added value perceived by custom-

FIGURE 2: The BCG Portfolio Analysis

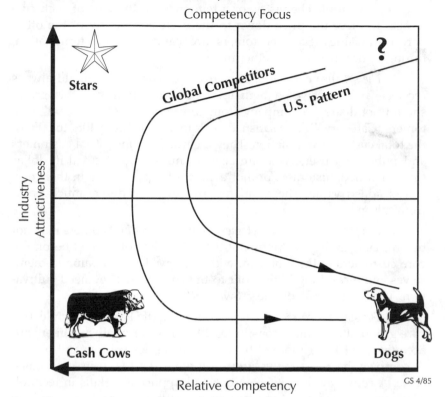

Competency Focus

Stars

Global Competitors

U.S. Pattern

?

Industry Attractiveness

Cash Cows

Dogs

Relative Competency

GS 4/85

ers. The two axes create four customer categories—each requiring a different corporate strategy.

1. *The "dog" customers.* Referring to customers as dogs is in poor taste. But there are always, in truth, several customers that are not worth keeping. In their article "Customer Satisfaction Fables" (*Sloan Management Review*, Summer 1994), Dawn Icabucci, Kent Grayson, and Amy Ostram state: "The briefest inquiry to any sales force will confirm that some customers are uninformed, unrealistic, and demanding. Most businesses have certain segments of customers who are not profitably worth satisfying." Even if customers are not hostile, there is at least 10% of the total customer population that is not profitable to a

company for a variety of reasons. These reasons may include low volume, incompatible chemistry, or a tendency on the part of such customers to drive the price down to the exclusion of any of the other perceived values. Such customers are candidates for termination, through price increases or other means.

2. *The satisfied customers.* This group of customers should always receive—and perceive—a high level of satisfaction, but this group should not distract a company from concentrating on its "core" customers (Category 4). The satisfied customers constitute 40% to 50% of the total customer population. They include both industrial customers and public end users, who are large in numbers but small in dollar sales. Satisfied customers do not expect a large increase in their perceived added value. The company also does not derive much profit from this group.

3. *The potential "core" customers.* This group of customers may not be profitable in the short term but they have the potential of becoming core customers in the long run, with perceived added value to themselves and a resulting high profit to the company. They need cultivation. They can be called "the growables."

4. *The star or "core" customers.* Following the Pareto principle, this core group of customers constitutes 20% or fewer of all customers but accounts for 80% or more of the company's sales volume and profits. A company best serves this group by what it adds to its customers' *value.* A company uses its expertise and application skills in technology, quality, cost, cycle time, people empowerment, and so on to help its customer companies become more competitive and more profitable in one or more of these areas. The added value that its customers perceive must be so continuously nurtured that it creates customers for life. They can be called "the already growns." It is this group of core customers on whom this briefing concentrates.

"Platinum, Gold, Silver, Bronze, and Tin" Customers

A. T. Kearney uses a metal analogy to differentiate and segment the customer base and the levels of products and services provided (*The Customer Satisfaction Audit*, Strategic Directions Publishers, Ltd., 1994). Some of the services provided may not be valued by some groups of

FIGURE 3: The Customer Portfolio Analysis

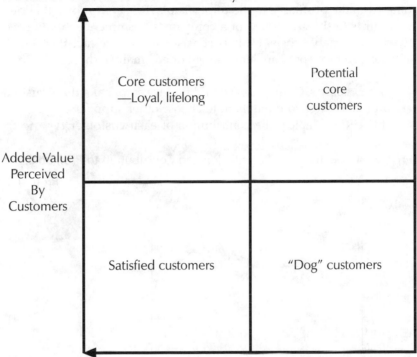

customers—thus driving up costs with no tangible benefit—while providing service levels too low for other groups.

Platinum customers. These are customers who receive maximum value from a company, and the company profits most from them. The company creates strategic alliances with them, which merge quality and productivity processes into a seamless, single process for both customer and supplier. (This not only increases profitability for both, but also increases the customer's threshold cost of moving to a new supplier.)

Gold customers. These are customers that are almost as important as the platinum customers, but they do not merit the creation of strategic alliances.

Silver customers. For these customers, a company provides differentiated packages of products and services. Relationships are at least maintained, if not assiduously cultivated.

Bronze customers. For these customers, a company finds itself slipping from the profitable to the unprofitable. Research shows that only two-thirds to three-quarters of a company's customers actually cover fixed and variable costs. (This is consistent with the fact that 30% to 40% of product costs are non-value-added, mainly the cost of poor quality.)

Tin customers. Companies should find ways to make these customers profitable or encourage them to choose other suppliers.

FIGURE 4 depicts the contribution of each customer type to the

FIGURE 4: Customer Differentiation and Contribution to Profitability

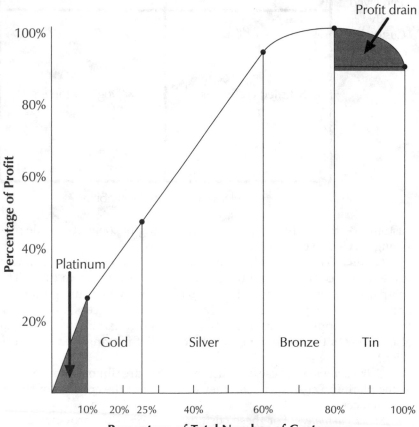

overall profit of a supplier company. Platinum customers, who comprise 10% of a company's total number of customers, contribute 25% to the overall profit; gold customers, 15% of the total number, contribute 25% to the overall profit; silver customers, 35% of the total number, contribute 45% to the overall profit; bronze customers, 20% of the total number, contribute only 5% to profit. Finally, tin customers, 20% of the total number of customers, actually *drain profits* by 15%.

The Internal Customer—"If Not a King, at Least a Prince"

There is a level of customer different from the categories of customers cited above: the internal customer. Companies respect—if not worship—their external customers, especially the core customers. But the internal customers—the next operations that receive the work of previous processes, be they business processes or design processes or manufacturing processes—are often treated like dirt! There is little love lost between an internal customer and an internal supplier in the interminable turf wars that go on between departments. As an example, manufacturing and engineering divisions in a company are often at loggerheads, even though manufacturing is engineering's most important internal customer. Engineering often considers manufacturing to be a second-class citizen, and tosses a half-baked product over the wall— with the timer ticking—for manufacturing to catch and muddle through.

In the new age of customer satisfaction and loyalty, the internal customer must be elevated to a high status—if not to that of a king, as is the external customer, then at least to that of a prince. Every process, be it a product or a service, has an internal customer whose requirements must be assessed as the external customers' are. Likewise, internal customer feedback and measurements should be sought. These evaluations should be more important than performance appraisals by the boss. In progressive companies, internal customer appraisals are replacing boss appraisals in determining merit increases and promotions. Sometimes, the internal customer can terminate the internal supplier for continued substandard performance—and, in extreme cases, even go outside the company for such service.

Peripheral Customers

Beside external and internal customers, a company has other peripheral customers who cannot be neglected.

Former customers: These dropouts must be identified. Their reasons for leaving the company must be scrutinized and a monumental effort made to win them back, especially if they are in the core group.

Noncustomers: Many companies neglect this key group. Attempting to analyze why noncustomers stay away from a company can go a long way in enticing them. Some of the more common reasons are: lack of knowledge of the company or its products; lack of advertising; price; poor public image (unfavorable media publicity); dissatisfaction with one element in a supply chain (e.g., not choosing a manufacturer because of an unfavorable experience with a distributor); and the bad-mouthing of friends and relatives.

Other stakeholders: A company has several stakeholders in addition to customers. Suppliers, distributors, dealers, and stockholders are, in a larger sense, customers who should be served. Sometimes, these stakeholders are taken for granted. Universities and other educational institutions pay scant attention to students as customers. They pay even less attention to industry, who hires their "product," or to parents, who pay them. In hospitals, doctors do not look upon their patients as customers, nor do administrators and other support staff.

The public: Finally, a company has an obligation to serve not only its stakeholders, including customers, but the public as well. Since a company derives its ultimate legitimacy from the community and the country in which it operates, its customers-at-large are, indeed, the public. Public perceptions of a company as a corporate citizen—in terms of integrity, employment, nondiscrimination, and environmental and social responsibility—are important attributes of its character, its citizenship, and its usefulness to society. A company that loses its public image, its public trust, is likely—and deserves—to go out of business.

3

Why Companies Don't Satisfy Their Customers

"Sixty-two percent of companies do not consider customer satisfaction a top priority."

—Learning Dynamics, Inc.

Despite the Hype of Customer Satisfaction, It's Mostly Benign Neglect

Why is it that, with a constant drumbeat in the media about the importance of customers and their pivotal roles in shaping a corporation, so many companies fail to satisfy them? Before cataloging the reasons for the lack of a customer focus, let us examine the dimensions of customer neglect among many companies.

A Customer Commitment Survey

Learning Dynamics, Inc. recently conducted a customer commitment survey among a large number of companies. Its findings, reported in J.K. Cannie and D. Chapman's book, *Keep Customers for Life* (AMA-COM, 1991) included the following:

- In 62% of the companies, not everyone is aware of what customers do with the company's product or service.

- Surprisingly, 62% do not consider customer satisfaction a top priority.
- Only 60% base their competitive strategy on attention to customer needs.
- Only 57% rate meeting customer needs as their number one priority.
- Fewer than half of new products and services are developed or improved based on customer suggestions and complaints, despite an MIT study which indicates that 80% of technological innovations—and the best innovations—come from customers.
- In 17% of the companies, not even salespeople talk to customers; 22% of senior management, 29% of marketing, and 67% of R&D do not talk to customers either.
- Regretfully, 13% have no one in their organization to represent the customer's point of view or act as the customer's advocate.
- Moreover, 12% use no formal methods to determine customer wants.
- Only 3% make customer satisfaction the number one criterion for determining senior managers' compensation.

These are grim statistics. A company that does not focus on customer satisfaction will not even qualify for the finals in world class competition, despite its attention to price and cost reduction, technology, product quality, or all three put together. And—if it persists in paying marginal attention to the customer—it is likely to end up on the ash-heap of corporate history.

Why Companies Do Not Focus on Customer Satisfaction

Corporations do not pay sufficient attention to customers and their satisfaction for a variety of reasons.

- They have little knowledge or conviction that the main objective of suppliers is to create and nurture satisfied, repetitive, and loyal customers who have received *added value* from their suppliers.
- They believe that they are in business to *make products* or render

services. But they seldom think that they are in business to *make satisfied, loyal, repetitive customers.*

- This limited horizon extends to employees as well. Employees label themselves in terms of their professions or tasks, but *almost never as customer satisfiers.* They call themselves data entry processors, salespeople, accountants, etc. Regardless of title, most still view customers either as a nuisance ("wouldn't it be wonderful around here if we did not have to deal with customers") or as nonentities ("customers are not my job").
- Many employees feel too removed from customers, not recognizing that they are links in a chain of customers, with the next operation as the immediate customer and the external customer at the end of that chain. (For a detailed examination of this topic, see K. Bhote, *Next Operations As Customer,* American Management Association Briefing, 1991.)
- Much too often products are developed by listening to the "voice of management" or to the "voice of the engineer," not the all-important "voice of the customer." In fact, management and engineers believe, in their hearts, that they know more about what customers want than the customers themselves!
- Company policies and procedures are designed for purposes of control and command, regardless of whether such policies are of little consequence to customers or—worse—would cause customer dissatisfaction.
- Customer contact employees—those frontline troops that interface frequently with customers—are not given the authority to go beyond company policy in accommodating customer concerns and complaints and diffusing their anger with adjustments, compensation, etc. The trained "smile" for customers, assiduously taught to employees, is pathetic in its inadequacy.
- It is almost an axiom that you cannot have happy customers without happy, productive employees. But the reason companies have indifferent, unmotivated employees has far, far less to do with the employees than with their overbearing, dictatorial, short-sighted management.
- Departmental walls and organization boxes often promote competition between factions jockeying for power, instead of cross-functional teamwork with a focus on customer needs and satisfaction.

Why Companies Do Not Incorporate
Customer Requirements Into Their Strategy

Even if they do not neglect their customers, companies nevertheless fail to incorporate what they know about customer requirements into their organization's overall strategy. There are four reasons for this:

1. Differences Between Customer Requirements and Company Perceptions

In one research project designed to determine how accurately customers thought suppliers understood their needs, *two-thirds of customers said they believed their needs were either seriously or somewhat misunderstood by their suppliers.* This was especially true for service elements, such as order processing, delivery cycle, and order receipt follow-up. In addition, in the area of identifying customer requirements, suppliers perceived "frequent contact with customers" to be far less important than did their customers. Further, over a fourth of companies did not systematically update their understanding of customer needs, or did so only once every two or three years.

2. Customer vs. Supplier Views on Meeting Customer Requirements

The perception gap in *understanding* customers' needs leads to a similar gap in *answering* needs. In general, customer perceptions of how well suppliers fulfill their needs are much lower than the corresponding perceptions of their suppliers. FIGURE 5 depicts several service factors in which the customer perceptions of the supplier's meeting their needs are *consistently lower*—by factors ranging from 2:1 to 10:1—than the equivalent supplier perceptions.

Even if a company understands what customers require to be totally satisfied and understands how its current performance measures up against those requirements, it may lack the commitment to achieve those targets and to create the perception in the minds of its customers that it is achieving those targets. Organizational disconnects, inappropriate skills, and various aspects of a company's culture can shortchange total customer satisfaction.

FIGURE 5: Customer vs. Supplier Views on Meeting Needs

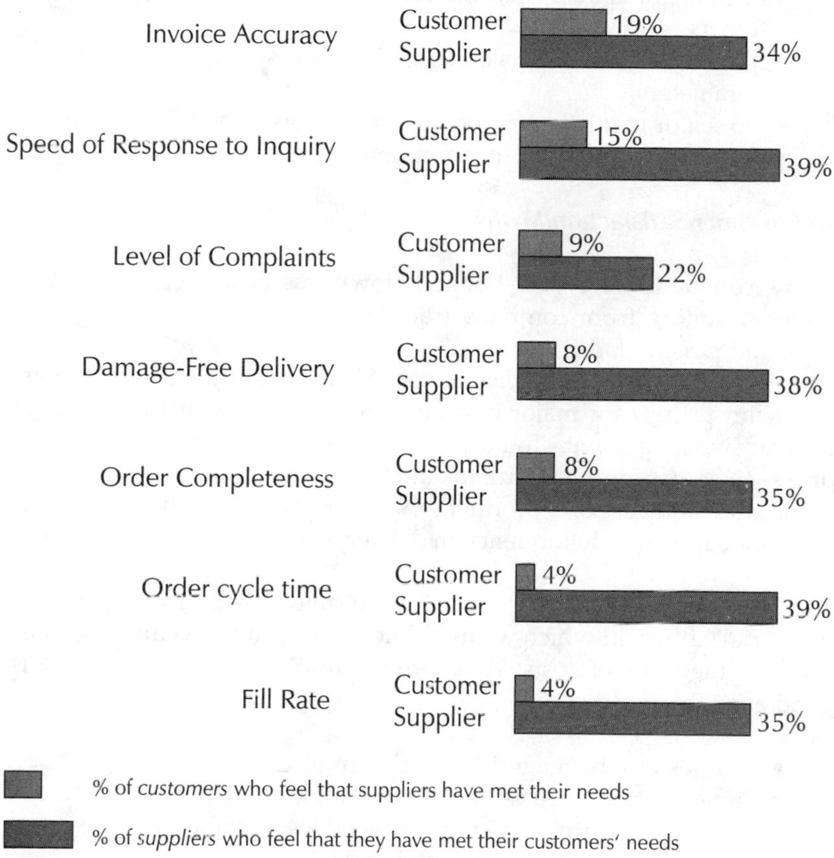

Invoice Accuracy	Customer	19%
	Supplier	34%
Speed of Response to Inquiry	Customer	15%
	Supplier	39%
Level of Complaints	Customer	9%
	Supplier	22%
Damage-Free Delivery	Customer	8%
	Supplier	38%
Order Completeness	Customer	8%
	Supplier	35%
Order cycle time	Customer	4%
	Supplier	39%
Fill Rate	Customer	4%
	Supplier	35%

▇ % of *customers* who feel that suppliers have met their needs

▇ % of *suppliers* who feel that they have met their customers' needs

3. Lack of Management Commitment to Customer Satisfaction

A few typical management practices are symptomatic of the lack of commitment to customer satisfaction:

- There is pervasive concern with short-term financial improvement rather than long-term customer satisfaction.
- Internal disagreements abound—between marketing and engineering, sales and production, or management and employees.

- Senior executives are not personally involved in customer satisfaction, nor is their financial compensation tied to satisfying customers.
- Monthly reviews focus on financial figures and not on customer parameters.
- No senior manager is appointed as the focal point for customers.
- A customer loyalty steering committee is not established.

4. Customer Satisfaction Myths

Many companies are still bogged down by customer satisfaction myths, resulting from company tradition, management shortsightedness, and passing fads.

"Price is the only thing that matters." It is amazing how this obsession with price, as a major customer focus, persists in the minds of company management. Today's customers are driven by value, not price—they want more "bang for the buck." To the sophisticated customer, the total cost of a product or service—which includes the costs of poor quality and delinquency in delivery—is becoming more important.

The 99-percent syndrome. In the "zero defects is a utopian dream" industrial culture in which we live, defects are condoned and even justified on the basis of costs. What are the implications of this "99% is good enough" mind-set?

- Airlines lose baggage 1.1% of the time.
- Restaurant bills are wrong 1% of the time.
- Doctors' prescriptions are incorrect 0.8% of the time.
- Payroll operations make mistakes 0.6% of the time.
- Wire transfers are wrong 0.6% of the time.
- Journal vouchers are incorrect 0.5% of the time.

Would we tolerate such errors in our personal lives? For another perspective, remember that there is only a 1% difference in the DNA genetic codes between a chimpanzee and a human being!

The pursuit of quality for its own sake. Even a 100% quality score—zero defects—is not enough if it is not accompanied by the twin imperatives of maximum customer satisfaction/loyalty and respectable profits for the company. In the 70-year-long history of modern quality control, the movement has lurched from fad to fad, each claiming to show the way to the promised land of perfection.

- In the 1950s, it was fascination with sampling plans.
- In the 1960s, it was the hoopla of the zero defects movement.
- In the 1970s, it was the lure of quality circles, transplanted from Japan.
- In the 1980s, it was the "fatal attraction" of statistical process control and control charts.
- In the 1990s, it is the forlorn hope of salvation with total quality management (TQM).

The disillusionment with TQM, discussed in Chapter 4, has become especially prominent in recent years. Consider several examples.

Several years ago, Florida Power and Light won the Holy Grail of quality awards—the Deming Prize. Several months later, it almost went broke. While its employees were forced into updating scores of quality charts, its customers were complaining about its poor service and blackouts during the peak of winter. A new management had to scrap many quality pursuits to focus on the customer.

Varian Associates concentrated on the quality of its products. "All of our quality-based charts went up, but everything else went down," lamented Richard M. Levy, executive vice president for quality. Customer concerns took a back seat and Varian went from a profit gain to a profit loss.

Wallace Co. filed for Chapter 11 bankruptcy soon after winning the Malcolm Baldrige National Quality Award, partly as a result of a business slump and customer neglect.

A few years ago, United Parcel Service concentrated on fast delivery as its most important quality strategy. It even redesigned the seats in its delivery vans to enable its drivers to get out faster! But sales sagged. UPS discovered that customers really wanted to interface with its harried drivers, ask questions, and receive guidance. UPS changed its focus, allowing its drivers to spend more time with its customers and even provided financial incentives to them when they generated more business. As a result, sales and profits shot up.

The moral of these mishaps is that "the pursuit of quality, per se, is no virtue; the pursuit of quality for customer satisfaction and profit is no vice."

The Unacceptable Costs of Dissatisfied Customers

A recent study by *Fortune* magazine and the Forum Corporation found several arresting facts.

- Satisfied customers will tell an average of five other people about their positive experiences with a company's product or service.
- The average dissatisfied customer, however, will tell nine other people about a negative experience with a company's product or service.
- But 13% of dissatisfied customers will broadcast their unhappiness with a company's product or service to 20 others!
- And, worst of all, 98% of dissatisfied customers never complain—they just switch to a competitor!

The cost of customer defections is monumental:

- not only because of their numbers today, but also because of the loss of these customers over their lifetime;
- not only because they broadcast their own disenchantment with the company, but because they may turn other potential customers into noncustomers;
- not only because of the loss of such sales but because of even greater profit loss, since long-term customers generate much higher profits than one- or two-time customers.

A Company's Best Friends and Worst Enemies

Thomas O. Jones and W. Earl Sasser, Jr., in a landmark article entitled "Why Satisfied Customers Defect" (*Harvard Business Review*, November-December 1995) distinguish four types of customers: loyalists, defectors, mercenaries, and hostages.

Loyalists are customers who are *completely* satisfied (a 5 on a scale of 1 to 5) and keep returning to the company. Loyalists constitute a company's bedrock. There is a perfect fit between their needs and the company's offerings. Within the loyalist group are those whose experiences so exceed their expectations that they become missionaries or *apostles* for the company.

Defectors generally give a company a rating of very dissatisfied, dissatisfied, or neutral (a score of 1, 2, or 3 on a scale of 5). Even a significant percentage of satisfied customers (who give a score of 4) become defectors the moment the competition offers a lower price or other perceived benefits. These customers account for 10% to 50% of the company's customer base.

Letting such customers defect is perhaps one of the worst mistakes managers can make. Showering attention on them when problems strike can convert at least 50% of them to loyalists. Within the defector group, the most dangerous are the *terrorists*. These are customers who've had bad experiences with the company. But the company does not listen or respond to them and does not correct their problems. As a result, they can't wait to tell others about their anger or frustration.

Mercenaries are satisfied customers who display no loyalty. They chase low prices, buy on impulse, pursue fashion trends, or seek change for the sake of change. They are expensive to acquire, yet quick to depart.

Hostages are those customers who experience the worst of a product or service but have no other place to go because the company operates in a monopolistic environment. Companies consider them captive. But at the first loosening of this monopolistic stranglehold, hostages escape. And in the meantime, they complain loud and long, devastating company morale.

How companies can meet the challenge of dealing with these diverse groups is the subject of the next chapter.

4

Customer Loyalty—The Ultimate Business Challenge

"Customer Satisfaction is but a milestone on the long, hard road to customer loyalty and lifelong retention. Customer loyalty is the flip side of the same coin called company profit."

—Keki R. Bhote

Customer Satisfaction—Poor Correlation with Bottom-Line Improvement

Conventional wisdom, supposedly learned from the Japanese, states that if a company assures customer satisfaction, its profits will take care of themselves. Flying in the face of this conventional wisdom, however, is a recent survey conducted by the renowned Juran Institute; as stated in the Introduction and repeated for emphasis here, it found that:

- A full 90% of top managers from over 200 of the largest corporations in America were convinced that "maximizing customer satisfaction maximizes profitability and market share."
- Yet fewer than 30% were confident that economic value had been added as a result of their customer satisfaction efforts.
- *And fewer than 2% were able to measure a bottom-line improvement from documented increases in levels of customer satisfaction.*

Customer Loyalty—The New Testament

It is now becoming apparent that it is no longer customer satisfaction but *customer loyalty that is the dominant key to business success.* Customer loyalty means that customers are so delighted with a company's product or service that they become enthusiastic word-of-mouth advertisers. Further, they extend their loyalty not only to that product or service, but also to the whole portfolio of the corporation's products and services for the better part of their lifetime—in short, brand loyalty forever.

FIGURE 6 shows the relationship between customer satisfaction and customer loyalty. The correlation between the two is very weak. A high customer satisfaction rating is no predictor of customer loyalty. A study conducted in the appliance industry indicated a respectably high customer satisfaction rating of more than 90% for almost all manufacturers, but the corresponding loyalty rating barely reached 50%, even for the best manufacturers.

By contrast, FIGURE 7 shows the very strong correlation between customer loyalty, as measured by retention rates, and corporate

FIGURE 6: Customer Satisfaction Is Not a Predictor of Customer Loyalty

FIGURE 7: Correlation Between Customer Loyalty and Profitability

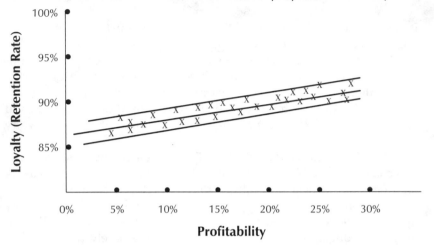

profitability. This figure underscores the main business reason that the *old testament* of mere customer satisfaction must give way to the *new testament* of customer loyalty and retention: *It is profit, profit, and more profit.*

From Zero Defects to Zero Defections

The quality movement has long stressed zero scrap and zero defects as essential ingredients of manufacturing. But companies should be even more concerned with scrap in its larger dimensions—customers who do not come back. Companies must move from zero defects to *zero customer defections* as the sine qua non of their existence!

It is now becoming an axiom among business experts and academicians that customer retention is not only a profit generator, but also that its contribution to profitability is much greater than that granted by the old gods of scale, market share, cost reduction, and new products.

A Profit Increase for Each Year of Customer Retention

If customers find *complete* satisfaction—a rating of 5 on a scale of 1 to 5—they generate more profit each year they stay loyal to a company.

In an excellent article entitled "Zero Defections: Quality Comes to Services" (*Harvard Business Review,* September-October 1990), Frederick F. Reichheld and W. Earl Sasser, Jr., cite the example of credit card companies that spend $51, on average, to recruit a new customer. FIGURE 8, drawn from that article, shows the profit generated per customer over time. The first year is still a net loss, but the profit per customer keeps increasing for each additional year, yielding a profit gain of over $100 per customer after five years. The authors replicated this trend in each of more than 100 companies in two dozen industries. For one industrial distributor, net sales per account continued to rise into the nineteenth year of the relationship!

FIGURE 8: Profit Generated Over Time per Customer: Credit Card Companies

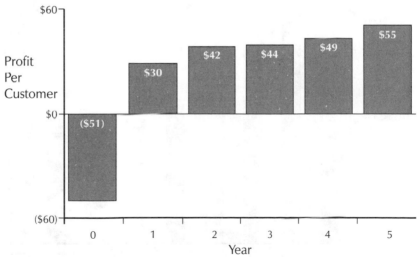

The Strong Correlation between Reductions in
Customer Defections and Profit Increases

Reichheld and Sasser have also studied the dramatic effect of reducing defection rates on a company's relationship with its customers and on its profits. FIGURE 9, drawn from the article previously mentioned, depicts the profit increases resulting from a 5% reduction in customer defections in various businesses. The profit increases by type of service vary from a respectable 30% up to a whopping 85%. MBNA America,

FIGURE 9: Profit Increases With a 5% Reduction in Customer Defections

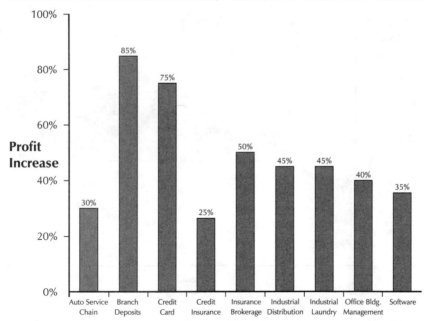

a Delaware-based credit card company, found that a 5% reduction in its customer defection rates increased its profits by more than 125%!

The Xerox Principles

Xerox is noted not only for the product innovations that it has given to the world, but also for managerial innovations, such as benchmarking and supply management. In the customer arena, it has formulated a set of principles that is equally revolutionary:

1. High quality products and associated services designed to meet customer needs create high levels of customer satisfaction.
2. This high level of customer satisfaction leads to greatly increased customer loyalty.
3. Increased customer loyalty is the single most important driver of long-term financial performance.

Xerox found that its *totally* satisfied customers were six times more likely to repurchase its products over a span of 18 months than its merely satisfied customers!

How the Competitive Environment Affects the Satisfaction-Loyalty Relationship

In "Why Satisfied Customers Defect" (*Harvard Business Review*, November–December 1995), Thomas O. Jones and W. Earl Sasser, Jr., examined over 30 companies in five markets with different competitive environments and different types of customer relationships. The five markets were automobiles, personal computers purchased by businesses, hospitals, airlines, and local telephone services. The metric for customer loyalty was the customers' stated intent to repurchase products and services. (Even though not all customers will follow through on their stated intent to repurchase, a minimum of 50% will do so. Other measures of actual repurchasing behavior include recency, frequency, amount, retention, and longevity.) FIGURE 10 depicts the influence of varying degrees of competitive forces on the satisfaction-loyalty relationship.

FIGURE 10: Influences of Degree of Competition on the Satisfaction-Loyalty Relationship

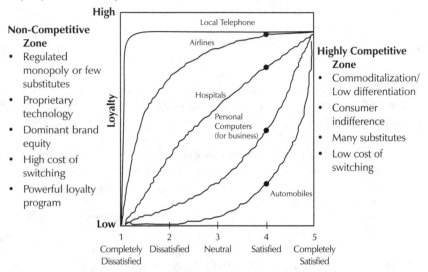

To analyze the impact of the competitive environment on these ratios, Jones and Sasser looked at two poles in the competitive continuum, as shown in FIGURE 10. The characteristics of highly competitive markets are:

- the availability of alternative products or services,
- the low cost to switch to the competition, and
- the availability of substitutes.

Banks, retail establishments, and hotels, for example, offer products or services that fall into this "commodity market" category.

The characteristics of non-competitive markets are:

- actual or virtual monopolies,
- regulated companies/industries,
- proprietary technology, and
- the near impossibility of switching to competition.

Electrical utilities, cable television companies, and transportation utilities with special rights of way fall into this near-monopoly group, as did telephone companies until the breakup of Ma Bell and the raiding of local telephone companies by long-distance carriers and vice versa.

Let's take a brief look at how the competitive environment impacts loyalty ratios for some common manufacturing and service providers.

1. **Automobiles:** *High competition.*
   Jones and Sasser studied 32 automobile models with data provided by the renowned J. D. Powers and Associates, who surveyed car owners one year after they had purchased their vehicles. *The study revealed a 1:4.5 ratio* in the loyalty of completely satisfied to just satisfied customers. The ratio was almost the same in several competitive service businesses.
2. **Personal computers (for businesses):** *Medium competition.*
   Jones and Sasser analyzed data from more than 2,000 business users of personal computers, provided by a J. D. Powers 1994 survey. The study showed a 1:2.25 ratio in the loyalty of completely satisfied vs. just satisfied customers. How can we explain the 50% higher relative loyalty of personal computer users in business compared to car buyers? The answer, simply, is that centralized purchasing and corporate standards erect barriers that prevent individual users from following their own preferences.
3. **Hospitals:** *Moderate competition.*
   The hospital data, provided by NCG Research—a company that measures service quality and customer satisfaction in the health care industry—was based on surveys of 10,000 patients treated in 82 hospitals in a wide range of locations in the United States. Here the ratio in the loyalty of completely satisfied vs.

just satisfied customers is only 1.25:1—only half of the corresponding figures for personal computers in businesses. Again, the reason is that the average patient finds it difficult to switch hospitals because the doctor, the HMOs, or other insurers often determine where these end users go for treatment.

4. **Airlines:** *Low competition.*
   The data for airlines, also provided by J. D. Powers, was based on a 1994 survey of 20,000 passengers who used the largest airlines and flew on 72 routes. FIGURE 10 indicates that there is only a minor difference in the relative loyalty of completely satisfied vs. just satisfied airline customers. This is because most people flying on a particular route base their decisions heavily on the time of departure and frequent-flier programs. These decisions "lock" a passenger in and thus create an artificial loyalty.

5. **Local telephone services:** *Virtual monopolies.*
   The data on local telephone services was provided by a "Baby Bell" company. It indicates that loyalty is virtually 100% regardless of any level of dissatisfaction or satisfaction. The near-monopoly of a local telephone service makes the user a virtual "prisoner" of the company.

The Potential for Radical Drops in Loyalty

The 400% to 600% drop in loyalty from the completely satisfied to the just satisfied customer is a fact of life in highly competitive markets. But there can also be radical drops in customer loyalty in the other markets. The shape of the noncompetitive curves in FIGURE 10 can easily snap into the shape of a competitive market curve under the right conditions—conditions that are becoming more and more prevalent.

In the business PC market, end users are exerting greater influence over their purchasing departments and corporate policies as one generation of PCs renders the prior generation obsolete.

In the hospital market, most hospitals still operate as if competition is absent and patients are not customers! But with the growth of HMOs and the radical changes taking place in Medicare and Medicaid plans in the United States, patients can switch doctors and—in the future—even switch HMOs or insurers.

The company that will leave its competition in the dust is the one that works on long-term customer loyalty, not just short-term customer satisfaction. Horst Schulze, president and COO of the Ritz-Carlton Hotels, a 1992 winner of the Malcolm Baldrige National Quality Award, stated: "Unless you have 100% customer satisfaction—and I don't mean that they are just satisfied but are excited about what you are doing—you have to improve. And even if you reach 100% customer satisfaction, you have to make sure that you listen just in case they change . . . so that you can change with them."

Despite this strong link between customer retention and customer profit and between *complete* customer satisfaction and customer loyalty, companies still live in "NATO" land—No Action, Talk Only! Companies may pay lip service to the importance of customers in vague and general terms, but their actions in retaining customers and capturing their loyalty lag woefully behind the rhetoric.

Corporate Myopia on Customer Retention

The REL Consultancy Group's survey on "Customer Retention and Corporate Profitability" explored specific business practices influencing retention among *Fortune* 500 companies. Listed below are some startling results, reflecting the tunnel vision of senior corporate executives regarding customer retention and loyalty.

Myopia #1: Defection rates. Half the survey participants reported a defection rate of at least 10%. One out of four reported a defection rate of at least 20%, and one out of ten a defection rate of at least 30%! (Actually, other surveys estimate a much higher *average* defection rate of 25%. Any company that exceeds a *maximum* defection rate of 10% [excluding truly unwanted customers] is headed for serious trouble.)

Myopia #2: Customer defection impact on sales. An unbelievable 61% of the participants felt that customer defections had an insignificant impact on sales. Worse, one in seven felt that customer defections would have *no* impact on sales!

Myopia #3: Action on defecting customers. More than one out of three participating companies did not even attempt to identify customers in danger of leaving. One out of four companies did not bother to ask defecting customers their reasons for leaving; and one out of three took no action regarding customers in danger of leaving.

Myopia #4: Customer retention as a measure of profitability. Only 17% of the companies used customer retention as a metric to improve profitability (even though 69% estimated that a 5% reduction in customer defections would have a significant impact on profitability).

Myopia #5: Fixation on cost reduction, new markets, and developing new products. By contrast, the most widely used measure for increasing profitability was cost reduction (23%); followed by identifying new markets (18%)—i.e., going after new customers and forgetting the old; followed by developing new products (18%).

Myopia #6: Major cause of customer defections. Extending this fixation on price, 27% of the companies felt that customer defections were predominantly price related and only 16% of those surveyed felt they were service related (even though it is recognized that service is at least twice as important as product and price to most customers).

Balancing these uniform perceptions, however, the REL survey does register a few positive and encouraging trends.

Impact on profits by reducing customer defections. Of those surveyed, 81% felt that their companies could increase profits by addressing the avoidable reasons for customer defections. Further, 43% estimated a 1% to 5% profit increase, 25% of the respondents estimated a 5% to 10% profit increase, and 12% felt there would be more than a 10% increase in profits. (Heartening as these perceptions are, the profit potential of retaining customers is estimated by experts to be much higher—a whopping 50% increase!)

Understanding of relationship between customer defection rates and profitability. A full 76% understood the tie-in between customer defection rates and profitability—23% understood specifically and quantitatively, while 53% understood it intuitively but not specifically.

Customer retention—A higher priority in the next five years. A total of 78% of the participants expected customer retention to become a higher priority in the next five years.

Customer loyalty a target in sales and marketing programs. Of all participants, 92% felt that maintaining customer loyalty was a factor in targeting sales and marketing programs, with 40% agreeing specifically and quantitatively and the other 52% agreeing intuitively but not specifically.

Keys for Customer Loyalty and Retention

Part 2 of this briefing details a seven-step roadmap that leads to enhanced customer loyalty and retention. A few key measures are listed here for emphasis and later elaboration.

- A top management conviction that the main objective of the company is to add *value* for a customer—by improving the quality, cost, cycle time, service, competitiveness, or profit, or a combination of several of these items.
- Making customer loyalty and retention a key long-term strategy.
- Appointing a chief customer officer (CCO), who should be second only to the CEO in importance, to officially represent the customer's point of view within the company. If a company can have a CEO (chief executive officer), COO (chief operating officer), and CFO (chief financial officer), why not a CCO? A mere ombudsman will not do.
- Having *all* senior managers spend at least 20% to 25% of their time with "core" customers.
- Making customer retention as important as goal achievement and sales growth in determining the compensation of senior managers.
- Creating happy, productive employees through real empowerment—not just token empowerment, as happens in most companies that mouth it—as the best way to create and retain happy customers.

Before we look at that roadmap, however, we need to establish a "compass"—a series of principles that point the company and its leadership in the right direction. This is the subject of the next chapter.

5

The Ten Inviolate Principles of Customer Loyalty

"What does it profit a man if he gains the whole world, but loses his soul?"

—the Bible

Principles—A Bedrock of Relationships, an Anchor of Stability

Principles have governed relationships among people, societies, religions, and countries for more than 5,000 years of civilization. They represent an anchor of faith and stability in a changing and uncertain world. They provide a moral compass for people to steer by.

It is essential, therefore, that customer loyalty be governed by a set of unchanging, steadfast principles that can cement a long-term marriage between a company and the public in whose realm it operates, and between a company and its core customers.

Principle 1: A Partnership Based on Ethics and Uncompromising Integrity

In today's world, corporate ethics seem as troubled as individual ethics. Stories of companies cited for financial skullduggery, bribes, kickbacks, and environmental violations fill the news media. These firms may get by—even win out—in the short run, but they lose their corporate souls and their very existence in the long run. A corporation with uncompromising integrity is not only successful over time but is held up by the public and by other companies as a role model.

"It's a fairly new realization for corporations," says crisis communications consultant Karl Fleming, president of Prime Time Communications, "but the right ethical decision is also the right business decision." This assertion, quoted by Bennett Daviss in "Revival of the Fittest" (*Ambassador*, December 1995), makes an important point: A confluence of events has rewritten the rules of the marketplace, regardless of whether companies understand this or not. "Every corporation is now doing business in a moral universe," according to Stride Rite chairman Arnold Hiatt, a pioneer in the realm of ethical business practice.

Four factors have converged to channel corporations into ethical probity:

- First, the public is beginning to judge companies by their social performance—their impact on the environment and their role in aggravating or relieving social problems—as much as by their financial performance.
- Second, consumers have become shell-shocked by a continuous barrage of reported shenanigans, both governmental and corporate in nature—from Watergate 24 years ago to Intel's cover-up of its flawed Pentium computer chips more recently.
- Third, crusading special-interest groups are exerting enormous pressure—from boycotts (against Mitsubishi for razing forests to meet Asia's demand for pulp) to congressional investigations (against tobacco companies)—on firms to toe the ethical line on social and environmental problems.
- Fourth, the competitive, unsparing, and technologically sophisticated media are motivating companies to be more honest. "A company's ethical lapse can now be flashed to news outlets and brokerage houses globally, before a CEO can hurry back from lunch," as Daviss put it in the article cited above.

Of course, the corporate world would be a better place if companies did not have to be pushed into honesty, empathy, and morality. Two sterling examples of corporate ethics and values at their best are Motorola, in the United States, and The Tata Group in India.

At Motorola, many years ago, a very lucrative contract for a multimillion dollar communication system with a Latin American government seemed to be in the bag, when the government's high-ranking procurement official asked for a kickback. Even though this was considered the norm for doing business with this country, Bob Galvin, the chairman of the board, issued a flat and firm edict that the company would rather lose business anywhere in the world than be a party to unethical practices. Today, the Motorola folklore is filled with anecdotes about Bob Galvin's uncompromising integrity and how he has promoted ethics as a top corporate value. Motorola's outstanding business success (its stock has appreciated 24 times in the last 11 years) and its reputation as one of the best-managed companies in the world are testimonial to the long-range economic value of ethics at its best.

The Tata Group, India's largest and most successful company, is a composite of over 100 businesses, each almost totally autonomous and each highly profitable. But it is the cement of the highest ethics and the most sensitive social conscience for its employees and for the public that holds the company together in a seamless web. It is the most admired company in India, and its reputation for honesty, empathy, and moral fiber is legendary in a country whose business community is noted for corruption.

Principle 2: Added Value in a Customer-Supplier Partnership

Principle 1 pertains mainly to a company's relationship with the public at large. The remaining nine principles deal more specifically with the relationship between a company and its core customers.

It is fashionable these days to speak of a win-win partnership between a company and its core customers. But most companies that claim such partnerships have not advanced them much beyond the slogan stage. The emphasis is still on "what's in it for me?" Principle 2 is a company's unshakable conviction that it exists to add true value to its core customers. That added value must be perceived by the customer in the form of improving its own performance. That improvement comes through the supplier's contribution to the customer company's quality, cost, cycle time, technology, and the like. These are advances that the company could not achieve by itself and so lead to greater competitiveness and higher profit for the customer. For the supplier, the quid pro quo is a loyal customer who contributes higher profits to it on a sustained, long-term basis.

By the same token, the core customer should respond with a reciprocal commitment to partnership with its key suppliers. This includes rendering active concrete help to them in such areas as quality, cost, and profitability where it may possess greater professionalism than the supplier. This becomes the surest vehicle for the customer company to help itself.

Principle 3: Mutual Trust: The Self-Fulfilling Prophecy

When a teacher looks upon students as stupid and incorrigible, they respond by fulfilling the teacher's lowest expectations. On the other hand, when a teacher has faith in the students, trusts them, and encourages them to reach for their highest potential, the students rise to the challenge. It's the principle of "the self-fulfilling prophecy."

Similarly, managers who do not trust their employees and have little faith in their ability or effort find themselves supervising sullen employees whose work ethic attests to the managers' low expectations. The employees' trust in the managers is equally low. True leaders trust their people, have faith in their creativity, and encourage them to grow to their full potential.

In his book *Idea of Ideas* (Motorola University Press, 1991), Bob Galvin relates that his father, Paul Galvin, who founded Motorola, "subjected me to a fierce discipline. He trusted me!" Trust begets—both in the manager and in the employee—a strong compulsion to live up to that trust. So it is with a company and its core customers. Trust is a logical outgrowth of principles and ethics. It takes time to build. It is a step-by-step iterative process, but it is enduring in terms of the loyalty that it engenders on both sides.

Principle 4: "Open Kimono" Policy: Sharing Technology, Strategy, and Cost Data

The "open kimono" policy—a term first used at Xerox—is the epitome of trust. It means that a company is willing to open its books on its technology, on its corporate strategies, and on its cost data to its core customer—and the core customer is willing to do the same. Very few companies have graduated to this level of trust and openness, but it is the essence of true partnership. For all practical purposes, the company is an extension of the core customer—except for ownership and finance. The "open kimono" policy is yet another measure of unquestioning loyalty.

Principle 5: Mutual Active Concrete Help

The amount of active, concrete help rendered between customer and supplier companies is a distinct feature that differentiates successful partnerships (fewer than 10% of a company's customers) from those that are partnerships in name only.

In the quality arena, as an example, supplier certification has been blown up to be the magic wand for outstanding quality success. Customer companies audit their key suppliers once or twice a year and expect them to achieve very high levels of quality as a result. The great majority of such certified suppliers register barely a 50% improvement. For customer companies to effect a tenfold and even a hundredfold supplier quality improvement in one or two years—levels that are desperately needed for industry to be globally competitive—they must visit and help their partnership suppliers frequently—at least once a week—until substantial improvements are under way. (For an in-depth study, see K. Bhote, *Strategic Supply Management*, American Management Association, 1989.)

Customer companies must coach the suppliers in powerful tools for quality improvement, such as the design of experiments, multiple environment over stress tests, quality function deployment, poka-yoke, and the costs of poor quality. They must coach suppliers in tools for cost improvement, such as value engineering, group technology, and learning/experience curves. They must coach suppliers in tools for cycle time reduction, such as total productive maintenance, focus factories, pull vs. push systems, small lots with very short changeover time, and process flows. There may also be other coaching needed in management, organizational development, design, manufacturing, people empowerment, and the like. Such coaching entails not just classroom training, but also hands-on help. However, fewer than 1% of a customer company's so-called professionals are equipped to render such in-depth coaching.

On the supplier's side, there must be reciprocally active, concrete help. This includes early supplier involvement in design, value engineering ideas, cost targeting, and determining meaningful but mutually acceptable specifications—in short, in all areas where the supplier's expertise is greater than the customer's and which can lead to greater customer productivity, shorter design cycle time, more competitiveness, and higher profit.

The questions frequently asked are: Why should a customer company spend valuable time and human resources on coaching partnership suppliers? And why should suppliers spend their time and resources rendering concrete help to partnership customers? The answer to the first question is that it is the best way for a customer to help itself improve quality, cost, and cycle time by an order of magnitude. The answer to the second question is that it is the best way for the customer to perceive the supplier's added value to the customer and to realize greater profit for itself. Further, such reciprocal help is the essence of goodwill, partnership, and loyalty.

Principle 6: Action on All Elements of Customer Enthusiasm

FIGURE 11 represents a network of twenty elements that combine to produce customer enthusiasm *for products*. This is a formidable list of factors that can influence a customer. But which of these elements is the most important? The engineer would say "technical performance," the sales force would opt for "features," the quality professionals would select "quality," and so on. The answer is that no one element is more important than others at all times, in all places, for all customers. In varying degrees, however, they all add up to customer enthusiasm, customer delight, customer value.

My college students have dubbed one of my theories on customer enthusiasm "Bhote's Law." It states: (1) The most important elements of customer enthusiasm are those elements which the *customer stresses as important*. If these are missing from a product, they merit top management's urgent action. (2) The best way to determine what customers deem important is to ask them—through quality function deployment (QFD) and other techniques. For the core customer, this determination must be pinpointed even more specifically—on a one-on-one basis.

For example, the U.S. auto industry had dominated the American car market with a larger than 90% share until the early 1970s. But the public was disgusted with the quality of U.S.-made cars. The Japanese saw quality as their market niche and boldly invaded the U.S. carmakers' turf to capture up to 30% of that market. (Were it not for voluntary

FIGURE 11: Network of Elements In Customer Enthusiasm for Products

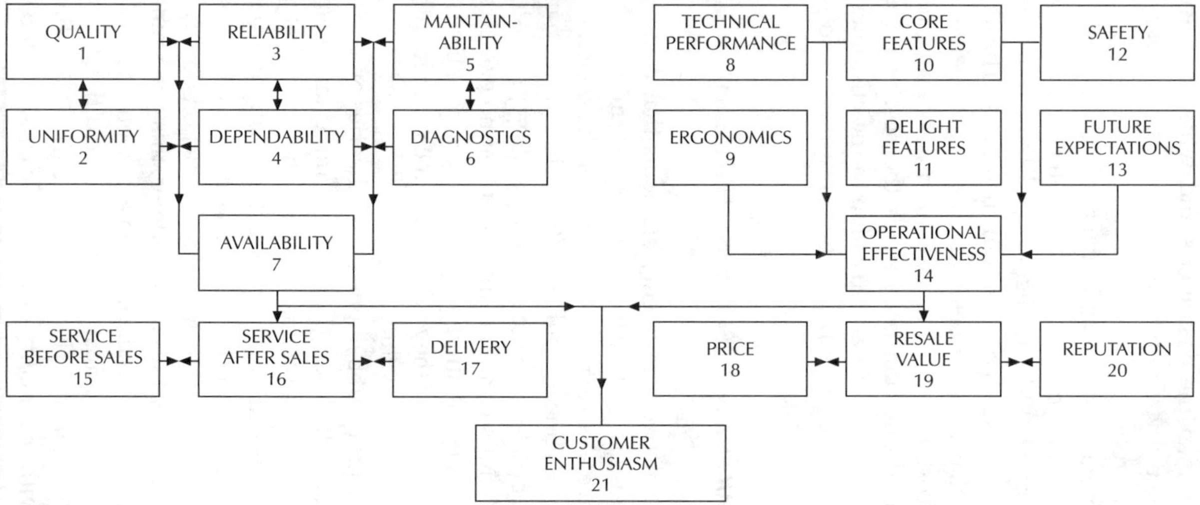

1. Quality: Toward Zero Defects
2. Uniformity: Toward Zero Variation
3. Reliability: Toward Zero Field Failures
4. Dependability: Toward Lifetime Guarantees
5. Maintainability: Toward Accurate, Fast, Low Cost Repair
6. Diagnostics: Toward Customer Self-Diagnosis
7. Availability: Toward 100% Up-Time
8. Technical Performance: State-of-the-Art Technology
9. Ergonomics: Styling, Color, Ease of Operation—"User Friendly"
10. Core Features: Expected by Customer

11. Delight Features: Unexpected Features That Thrill Customers
12. Safety: Of Product and to User Product Liability Prevention
13. Future Expectations: Anticipating Needs
14. Operational Effectiveness: Integration of Boxes 8 through 13
15. Service Before Sales: Sales, Cooperativeness, Communication
16. Service After Sales: Sustained Contact and Interest After Sales
17. Delivery: Short Cycle Time
18. Price: Cost Below Competition
19. Resale Value: High Percent of Purchase Price
20. Reputation: Image, Perceived Quality

21. CUSTOMER ENTHUSIASM: VALUE, DELIGHT, LOYALTY

restrictions on their part, the figure could have risen to 50%). Belatedly, the U.S. carmakers have moved to reduce the quality gap and, based on the J. D. Powers ratings, are recapturing at least 30% of the market share lost to the Japanese.

FIGURE 12 shows a similar network of elements that combine to produce customer enthusiasm in the service industry. The elements are somewhat different from those associated with products, but the approach is the same and Bhote's Law applies to services with equal validity.

FIGURE 12: A Network of Elements of Customer Enthusiasm—For Services

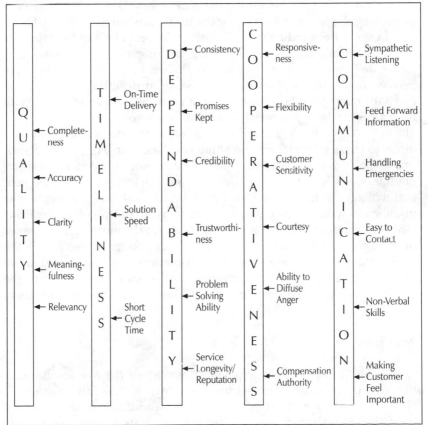

Principle 7: Focus on the Unexpected that Generates Customer Delight

In the battle to please customers, most companies do provide a core of features that the customer expects and gets. Quality, which is sometimes mistakenly equated with features, is also in the same league. Today, the rising expectations of the car buyer have reduced features and quality to a given. Customers are prevented from defecting but they are no longer excited. The latest trend is to develop some feature that the customers do not know about or anticipate, but which excites them when included. Here again, the Japanese carmakers have stolen a march on the U.S. car industry. For the last three years, Japanese car owners have had an electronic map locator that can tell them where they are and the best route to a particular destination. This is only now being talked about as a feature for the future among the U.S. Big Three.

In the service industry, the Sheraton Towers Hotel in Singapore is an excellent example of how offering the unexpected generates customer delight and subsequent loyalty. When you enter the lobby, the bellhop does not take you to the registration desk but directly to an assistant manager who, surprisingly, already knows your name. With no waiting in line, you are ushered into your room. Moments later, a "butler" comes in to check if everything is to your satisfaction, and offers to press your clothes and shine your shoes free of charge. Someone else brings in a whole complimentary case of toiletries. In the afternoon, a snack is served with your tea. You are invited to join the general manager in the evening for free cocktails and hors d'oeuvres. The night ends with a rich dessert served in your room before bedtime. Wake-up calls come with free tea or coffee and the morning newspaper of your choice. The staff on your floor greet you by name. That is the difference between mere customer satisfaction and customer delight! The payoff is the customer returning to the same hotel, despite the existence of more luxurious, but "cold" hotels with hardly a personal touch.

Principle 8: Closeness to the Customer

Konusuke Matsushita, the legendary founder of the Matsushita electronics empire, would counsel his sales force to "take the customer's skin temperature every day." There is no question that the bonds of trust that build up between a company and its core customers are largely based on the *close, personal relationships* between individuals in the two companies. This is not just friendship or favoritism; it is the confidence that each person is working to help the partner company for mutual benefit.

A survey for AT&T examined the factors involved in sales wins and sales losses. These included the complexity of the equipment, size of the orders, comparisons with the competition, characteristics of the account executive, the ratio of the number of account executives to technical advisors, and the like. The results, using a paired comparison technique, revealed that the greatest correlation to success was the amount of time spent with the customer and *the ensuing personal relationship of mutual respect and trust.*

Another perspective on closeness to the customer is *top management personally spending time with its core customers.* A 1988 survey by Learning Dynamics, Inc. revealed that 40% of senior managers spend less than 10% of their time with customers. (See J. K. Cannie and D. Chapman, *Keep Customers for Life*, AMACOM, 1991). By contrast, another 34% of senior managers do spend more than a fourth of their time with customers. What a bipolar distribution! Top management often loves to sit in its ivory tower, issuing mission statements and policies. While these are important, they are no substitute for getting out into the real world of their customers, where the action is.

Motorola's Bob Galvin again set the trend in 1986 when he personally selected and visited his top 10 customers. He did not meet with his counterpart CEOs but with the employees who actually "felt, smelt, and dealt" with Motorola's products. He spent a whole day with each customer and got unfiltered feedback. The visits were so rewarding that he institutionalized this procedure, requiring that every senior executive visit 10 top customers each year.

A similar effort, not only for core customers but also for individual end-users, conducted on a random basis, holds great promise for customer loyalty. One vice president of a large television company would select two households owning his firm's TV sets to visit each time he went out of town for business meetings. The impact on the homeowners was electrifying. "Can you imagine," they would excitedly tell their friends and neighbors, "a top VP of a multinational firm actually spent an hour of his valuable time with us, sincerely listening to our comments—good and bad—and took action!" This word-of-mouth communication proved to be more powerful than any advertisement in those communities!

From an organizational perspective, closeness to the customer requires that a member of the company's top management be formally appointed as the *customer's advocate within the firm.* A mere senior executive as ombudsman, a troubleshooter of customer complaints, is not good enough. If a company can have a COO (chief operating officer) and a CFO (chief financial officer), the least it can do is to *create a CCO (chief customer officer)* who would rank second in importance after the CEO. Yet according to the Learning Dynamics' survey cited above, only 7% of the companies reported having a CCO. In 41% of the companies, salespeople were the only ones representing the customer's point of view. In another 38%, the customer service representative was the lone voice of the customer.

Finally, from a human resources perspective, closeness to the customer must equate to closeness to employees. *It is almost an axiom that you cannot have happy customers without happy, productive employees.* That means giving employees, especially the frontline troops who come into frequent contact with customers, sufficient administrative, managerial, and financial freedom to deal with customers on the spot and backing them up in their decisions, even if that means added expense to the company. In a larger sense, it means giving employees not just token empowerment, as most companies seem to do, but real empowerment—as perceived by the employees themselves.

Principle 9: Genuine Interest in the Customer After the Sale is Consummated

A survey of car buyers who did not develop loyalty to their dealers and return to them for their next purchase revealed that

- 1% had died;
- 3% had moved to another city;
- 5% switched because of price;
- 9% switched to another car manufacturer; and
- 14% switched because of poor repair service.

That totals 32%. What about the remaining 68%? They switched because "the dealer didn't give a damn." The moral here is that loyalty is assured by never forgetting the customer, even long after the sale has been consummated. It is said that service to the customer is five times as important as price—and close attention to the customer after the sale is five times as important as service, in terms of long-term loyalty.

One car salesman who won a national reputation for selling twice as many cars as the second-best salesman calls his customers soon after the sale and periodically thereafter to solicit their reactions and help them. He calls them on their birthdays, alerts them for their next service check-up, helps them resolve any servicing problems, and even assists in the resale of their cars.

Enterprising grocery stores keep track of their regular customers, the frequency of their visits, the amounts they spend, their product selections, their favorite brands, etc. They inform these loyal customers of special items that are soon to go on sale, send out discount coupons, and above all get to know and greet them as friends. (Of course, all of this would not have been possible in the precomputer, preinformation technology age.) Such attention to the customer does cost time and money in a business with the slenderest of profit margins. But the return on investment on a typical loyal customer who spends $3,000 to $6,000 a year at the store makes it worth going the extra mile. Similar methodologies are coming into vogue at banks, insurance companies, hotels, airlines, and other service suppliers who can add value to their loyal customers.

Principle 10: Anticipation of Future Customer Needs and Expectations

It is one thing to determine the current needs of existing customers, but it is quite another to peek into the future and anticipate the changing needs of current customers, their unmet and even unknown future expectations. Fortunately, there are techniques that a company can use to polish its crystal ball with its core customers. The company can

- involve top management with the core customer's top management in business, market, and product strategy,
- institute a joint customer-supplier product or service planning process,
- start joint R&D projects with key engineering and marketing personnel from the customer company,

- organize roundtables, focus groups, and clinics using a small sample of the public likely to be the "center of gravity" of the target market, and
- benchmark best-in-class companies that have an established track record of anticipating customer needs and expectations.

There are critics who believe that there is not much usefulness in sharing a company's innovations with customers, especially with customers who may be totally unaware of such innovations or their practical applications. But major innovations and technical break-throughs are not an everyday occurrence. Going from vacuum tubes to transistors, from transistors to integrated circuits and microprocessors, and from mobile radios to cellular phones are examples of such break-throughs. But they occur only once or twice per decade. In the mean-time, there are hundreds of opportunities for new products and ser-vices that occur all the time, in a steady stream of smaller innovations where the customer's involvement is not only desirable but should also be eagerly sought. It is the difference between an occasional home run and a hit every time at bat.

It is well known that 80% of all new products in the marketplace are the result of customer ideas and suggestions. Consider, for in-stance, the service of a concierge in a hotel. For years, such services were confined to routine matters—road directions, airline confirma-tions, theater tickets. But customers have been expanding the horizons of a concierge—from hotels to office buildings; from routine services to meals, flowers, laundry, and many more services that the harried office executive is only too happy to pay for!

Part 2

A Seven-Step Roadmap to Attain and Maintain Customer Loyalty, With an Audit to Assess Effectiveness at Each Step

6

Step 1: Top Management Commitment and Involvement

"We have far too many managers running industry, but far too few leaders."

—John Kotter

The Infrastructure of a Customer-Oriented Culture

The preamble to customer loyalty is the unconditional and enthusiastic acceptance of the 10 principles of customer loyalty detailed in Chapter 5. But the entire company culture must also be changed from an internal focus of serving management to an external focus of serving the customer, from the drudgery of the workplace and TGIF (Thank God it's Friday) to joy in the workplace and TGIM (Thank God it's Monday)! A culture change, in turn, requires a change in the beliefs and values of the entire workforce. The beliefs and values of employees will only change with a paradigm shift in the way work and jobs are structured and in the way people are hired, trained, evaluated, compensated, and advanced. The difference between the traditional paradigm and the customer paradigm is shown in TABLE 2.

Top Management—The Alpha and Omega of a Company's Direction

"Nothing happens without top management support and involvement." That statement is more than a cliché—it is a fact of corporate

TABLE 2: A Shift from the Traditional Paradigm to a Customer Paradigm

Characteristic	Traditional Paradigm	Customer Paradigm
Work units	Functional departments	Process teams with customer focus
Jobs	Simple tasks; checking; monitoring	Multi-dimensional work; little check; trust
Employee roles	Controls; follows rules	Empowerment; making their own rules
Hiring	Skills; experience	Broad education; team spirit; character; initiative; self-discipline; customer sensitivity
Job enhancement	Training; increasing skills—teaching the *how* of a job	Education—increasing insights—teaching the *why* of a job
Job evaluation	Boss appraisal	Customer appraisal; impact on profitability of company
Compensation	Small merit increases, based on position in the organization, number of people managed	No routine merit increases, but bonuses; higher compensation
Advancement	Based on performance	Based on ability and leadership potential
Employee beliefs and values	• "Boss pays my salary" • "I'm just a cog in the wheel" • "The more direct reports I have, the	• "Customer pays my salary" • "Every job is important; I do make a difference" • "My importance is

Characteristic	Traditional Paradigm	Customer Paradigm
	more important I am" • "Tomorrow will be just like today"	based on my contribution to customer satisfaction" • "We must live with constant change—I must constantly learn"
Corporate culture	Drudgery, TGIF (Thank God it's Friday)	Joy in work, TGIM (Thank God it's Monday!)

life. Jay Sprechler, in his renowned book *When America Does It Right* (Independent Engineering Management Practices, 1988) examined the customer services of 56 companies named "most admired" by *Fortune* magazine. He states, "Without the CEO's attention, customer service can be neglected and wither away. There isn't a single case where customer service developed from a bottom-up approach. The CEO can never walk away from maintaining a direct, highly visible, and pervasive involvement."

Top management must lead the way. To transform the traditional paradigm into a customer paradigm, top management—as a starting point—must understand the vast financial potential of customer loyalty and retention. This should be followed by several actions.

1. Create a customer loyalty steering committee, with no less a representation than the CEO and all direct reports. The committee's task should include, but not be limited to:

- Appointing a *"customer czar"* as the customer focal point; this person will be the customer's advocate within the company. Such a person should have the title of CCO (chief customer officer) and be second in rank after the CEO—ahead of the COO and CFO.
- Establishing a specific and quantifiable goal for customer defection. A target figure would be to hold defections to a maximum of 5% of core customers (excluding the termination of unwanted customers).

- Formulating *a customer retention mission statement*. A typical one could read, "To create and nurture loyal customers who have received—and perceived that they have received—added value from us; to retain their loyalty over many years; and to do all this in a manner that will lead them to share their positive experiences with others."

2. Quantify the lifetime value of a customer. Traditional accounting is seldom competent enough to capture the value of a lifetime customer. Curves can be generated, based on company history, that depict added value per customer per year as their defection rates are cut. FIGURE 13, developed by Reichheld and Sasser, shows a credit card company's defection rate of customers compared to customer value. The latter is the net present value of the profit streams a customer generates over the average customer life. At a 10% defection rate, for example, the average customer life is 10 years (1 divided by the 10% defection rate).

As the defection rate is cut from 20% to 10%, the average lifespan of the company's relationship with a customer doubles from five years to ten and the value of that customer (i.e., company profit) nearly doubles from $300 to $525.

3. Quantify the lifetime loss of a defecting customer. A study by the U.S. Office of Consumer Affairs indicates that 98% of unhappy customers do not complain. They switch companies—period—and tell, on average, nine of their friends and neighbors about their negative experience with the company. What is the lifetime damage to the company?

Cumulative loss of sales = average sales to a customer per year
x
number of customers lost per year
(the average is 25% of the customer base)
x
the average number of long-term purchases
+
the potential loss of sales from an average of half of the 9 friends of each lost customer

For a car dealership, with an average sale of $20,000, a loss of just 10 customers per year, and a loss of repeat business 10 times during a buyer's working lifetime, the defection loss can ratchet up to a stagger-

FIGURE 13: Company Profit (Customer Value) vs. Customer Defection Rate

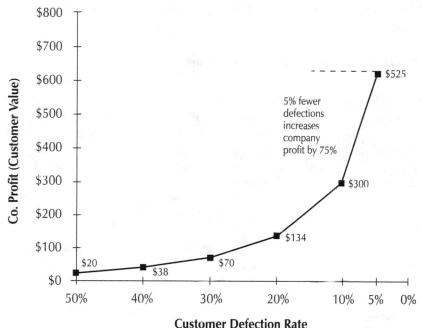

Customer Defection Rate

ing $2 million—not counting the potential turning away of friends and neighbors! Phil Bressler, the co-owner of five Domino's Pizza stores in Montgomery County, Maryland, calculated that a regular customer was worth more than $5,000 over the life of a 10-year franchise contract. Delta Airlines estimated that one lifetime customer is worth $1.5 million and Minute Maid estimated that one loyal customer provides $26,000 worth of free advertising by word of mouth alone!

4. Practice defections management. This involves a massive effort to anticipate potential customer defections; to analyze defections that have already occurred; and to lure most of the defecting customers back to the company. Management should consider the formation of a customer defection "SWAT team" to address these all-important defection issues. Defection management is discussed in greater detail in Chapter 12.

The Hen and the Pig: Support vs. Involvement

The difference between words and deeds, between mere top management support and its involvement, is illustrated by the old story of the hen and the pig, who wanted to reward the farmer for having taken such good care of them. They hit upon breakfast. The hen then brightly suggested ham and eggs. The pig protested. "Oh no," he said, "yours is support, mine is involvement."

One sure way to gauge the degree of top management involvement with the customer is to profile how these executives spend time each week. TABLE 3 separates the *amount of time top management spends on customer care* and the *time spent on activities unrelated to the customer*. If we assume that a manager's most irreplaceable resource is time, and if senior managers devote at least 20% to 25% of their time to customers, it is a tangible confirmation of the true value they attach to the customer.

TABLE 3: Profile of Hours per Week Spent by Top Management on Customer Care vs. Other Activities

1. Personal contacts with customers	_____*
2. Visiting customer-contact employees	_____
3. Determining what customers, former customers, and non-customers want	_____
4. Feedback from customers on company's performance	_____
5. Recognizing outstanding customer service employees	_____
6. Cutting costs	_____*
7. Meetings with other executives, managers	_____
8. Talking to stockholders, financial analysts	_____
9. Influencing technical improvements	_____
10. Policy and strategic planning	_____

*If the total hours in the first five items is greater than the total hours for the second five items, the CEO is voting for customer care with that most precious resource—TIME.

Values—A "Magnetic North"

Many CEOs spend a considerable amount of time in formulating values—or beliefs—for their corporations. These values are a "magnetic north," a compass, to guide the activities of all employees. But a number of CEOs stop after publishing these values. They become a wall-hanging. For values to have value, they must be lived and breathed by top management, disseminated to all employees, studied by them, and—more important—accepted by them.

An important way to gain employee acceptance is for top management to model the behavior it wants. Behavioral scientists state that behaviors are learned from past experiences, when such behavior has been rewarded or ignored or punished. A behavior that is followed by a reward is positively reinforced and likely to be repeated, whereas a behavior that is followed by punishment is strongly deterred and not likely to be repeated.

Demonstrating Customer Commitment to Employees

Employees easily pick up signals by which they can gauge whether top management truly pursues customer satisfaction and loyalty. These include:

- Paying attention to the *metrics* associated with customer satisfaction and especially customer loyalty (see Chapter 10).
- Maintaining *uncompromised integrity* in dealing with customers and the public.
- *Trusting in employees* and their ability to grow *as a reflection of trust in customers.*
- Taking strong and urgent corrective action on that element of customer satisfaction missing from the company's product.
- Personally spending time with customers.
- Committing resources—time, personal attention, and money.
- Giving customer-contact employees authorization to make their own decisions in dealing with customers—especially irate ones—even if it costs the company to do so.
- Rewarding those employees who provide excellent customer service and celebrating such achievers.
- Communicating the commitment to the customer in publica-

tions, advertisements, newsletters, news releases to the media, and in annual reports.

- Encouraging feedback from employees; publicizing and rewarding their ideas.
- Establishing customer satisfaction and loyalty as a key part of the agenda at periodic meetings.

Walking the Talk

Leaders can create and communicate a customer vision, devise a strategy to achieve that vision, and lead the process—and yet fail to achieve continuous improvement. What's missing is a focus on managing what matters to customers. The two critical elements of managing what matters are the right talk and the right walk. The talk is *what* a company must do to achieve its objective. The walk is *how* it turns its talk into reality. Brian Maguire, in his excellent article "12 Steps to Walking the Talk" (*National Productivity Review*, Autumn 1995) lists the steps management must practice:

1. Say what you're going to do in simple, concise steps.
2. Do what you say you're going to do.
3. Convince *influencers* to become *champions*.
4. Tell *stories* to connect employees to what matters, in their terms.
5. Put every improvement idea to the "what matters to customers" test.
6. Ask only for feedback you intend to act on.
7. Set boundaries, then get out of the way.
8. Fight "scope creep" and get closure.
9. Recognize and reward closure.
10. Make failure for the right reasons OK.
11. Make skeptics part of the *solution*.
12. Acknowledge the past and learn from it.

Notes on the Customer Loyalty Audit and Scoring System

Step one of the seven-step roadmap to attain customer loyalty follows. This step and all subsequent steps are presented in an audit format that allows a company to measure its effectiveness at each stage. This self-assessment is best initiated by a top management customer loyalty steering committee and executed by a cross-functional team, consisting of a member from top management—preferably the chief customer officer (CCO)—and members from sales/marketing, service, quality assurance and, especially, a representative from customer-contact employees.

Rating

The audit lists several success factors that contribute to the effectiveness of each step. Each success factor should be given a rating of 1 to 5 by the self-assessment team, with 1 being the worst and 5 being the best, using the following criteria.

Rating	Criteria
1	No knowledge of the success factor
2	Only a conceptual awareness of the success factor
3	Success factor started, with less than 50% implementation
4	Success factor 50% to 80% implemented
5	Success factor implementation over 80%; reflected improvements in customer loyalty metrics and business results

Step 1: Top Management Commitment and Involvement	Rating				
	1	2	3	4	5
A. Inviolate Principles of Customer Loyalty (Core Customers)					
1. *Perceived added value.* The company's core customers perceive that it has added value to their own operations—in terms of improved quality, cost, cycle time, innovations, technology, etc.—all leading to their greater competitiveness and profitability.					
2. The company is perceived by its core customers and the public as having uncompromising ethics.					
3. There is a climate of mutual trust between the company and its core customers that fuels a win-win partnership.					
4. There is an "open kimono" policy between the company and its core customers—a complete sharing of each other's technology, strategy, and cost data.					
5. The company renders active help to its core customers, including early involvement in design, value engineering ideas, and cost targeting.					
6. The company focuses on that element of customer satisfaction that is important to the customer and missing from its products or services.					
7. The company focuses on product or service innovations that customers do not expect but which delight them when introduced.					
8. Closeness to the customer is assured through developing close personal relationships and appointing a chief customer officer (CCO) as the customer's advocate.					

Step 1: Top Management Commitment and Involvement (cont'd)	Rating				
	1	2	3	4	5
9. The company displays genuine interest in the customer long after the sale is consummated.					
10. The company anticipates the customer's future and changing needs with joint R&D projects, focus groups, and clinics.					
B. A Paradigm Shift—From Traditional to Customer Focus					
1. Top management is moving away from functional departments to cross-functional process teams.					
2. Jobs are redesigned from simple, routine, boring tasks to multi-dimensional and self-checking, based on trust.					
3. Employees are encouraged to make their own rules and take on associated responsibilities and consequences.					
4. Hiring is based not on narrow skills, but broad education, team spirit, character, initiative, and customer sensitivity.					
5. Training is changed from the "how" of a job to the "why" of a job.					
6. Performance appraisal is changed from boss evaluation to customer (both external and internal) evaluation.					
7. Pay is changed from small, routine merit increases to performance bonuses.					
8. Promotion is changed from past performance to ability, creativity, and leadership potential.					

Step 1: Top Management Commitment and Involvement (cont'd)	Rating				
	1	2	3	4	5
C. Actions to Focus on Customer Loyalty and Retention					
1. A customer loyalty steering committee is established.					
2. A customer czar, or chief customer officer (CCO), is selected to be the customer focal point of the organization.					
3. A quantified, maximum customer defection limit is in place.					
4. A customer retention mission statement has been formulated.					
5. The lifetime value of a customer has been quantified.					
6. The lifetime loss of a defecting customer has been quantified.					
7. A customer defection "SWAT team" is in place to actively tackle customer defection issues.					
D. Management—Close to the Customer					
1. Top management officers spend a minimum of 25% of their time personally dealing with core customers.					
2. It visits its core customers at least once a year, spending time with the actual users of its products and services.					
3. It ensures that its senior executives visit their key customers, receiving feedback and suggestions from them.					

Step 1: Top Management Commitment and Involvement (cont'd)	Rating				
	1	2	3	4	5
4. It visits its customer-contact personnel, its field offices, and its service centers at least once per year for multinational companies and several times a year for smaller companies.					
5. It conducts management by wandering around (MBWA) among all its employees, listening to them, encouraging and supporting them, and acting on their ideas.					
6. It conducts rap sessions with small groups of employees to listen to their concerns, removing roadblocks that keep them from focusing on the customer.					
7. It not only shuts down a product line when quality or other characteristics adversely affect a customer, but encourages and authorizes all employees to do so if customer satisfaction is jeopardized.					
E. Behavior Reinforcement					
1. Top management reinforces adherence to customer satisfaction with recognition and awards to employees who enhance customer loyalty.					
2. Top management deters employee neglect or indifference to customers with appropriate disincentives.					
F. Demonstrating Commitment to Employees					
1. Top management has developed, implemented, and monitored a system of gauging customer satisfaction and loyalty.					
2. It supports its employees with resources, time, and personal attention to focus their energies on customer satisfaction.					

Step 1: Top Management Commitment and Involvement (cont'd)	Rating				
	1	2	3	4	5
3. It emphasizes those company policies and procedures that directly impact the customer and de-emphasizes (or even eliminates) those that are of no consequence to the customer.					
4. It authorizes contact employees to use their own discretion in dealing with customers, including financial compensation within guidelines.					
5. It encourages innovative ideas from employees in addressing customer issues and publicizes and rewards such ideas.					
6. It recognizes and rewards those employees who provide excellent customer service and celebrates their achievements throughout the company.					
7. It communicates its commitment to the customer in all its publications—newsletters, video tapes, bulletins, and quarterly and annual reports.					
8. It establishes customer satisfaction and loyalty as a key agenda item at its periodic review meetings, even elevates the item to first place on the agenda.					

7

Step 2: Internal Benchmarking—A Baseline

"Benchmarking without a firm measurement of your own company's status is a ship afloat without an anchor."

—from a Motorola Internal Publication

Know Yourself Before You Know Your Competition

Once a company decides that customer loyalty is its most important objective, and once its top management has made an unequivocal commitment to pursue that objective, it must determine its current status. Where, exactly, is the company positioned on the road to customer loyalty?

Benchmarking, a major corporate discipline developed in the past 15 years, provides an excellent means for determining that position. The first step is to conduct an *internal* benchmark study. The results can be used to determine the gap between a company and its benchmark partner and as a baseline for further improvement. (For a definitive review of benchmarking, see Michael Spendolini, *The Benchmarking Book*, AMACOM, 1992.)

This chapter is designed to help a company conduct an internal benchmarking. It is divided into the major categories of a company's activities, starting with measurement and then assessment of its management, people, organization, systems, tools, design, suppliers, manufacturing, field operations, and support services.

Measurement

Chapter 10 details several metrics to assess customer satisfaction and loyalty. The most important areas that should be measured to determine current performance include:

- *Customer loyalty*: the number and percentage of loyal customers and their longevities.
- *Value added to core customers*: money saved for core customers, *as measured by the core customers*.
- *Cost of poor quality*: not just the costs of scrap, rework, and warranties, but the entire array of hidden costs.

Although the cost of poor quality is used mainly as a total quality management (TQM) metric, this measure integrates the failings of management, human resources, products, and services. FIGURE 14 depicts several elements associated with the cost of poor quality. Like an iceberg, where only the tip shows and the greater portion is submerged out of sight, a mere 20% of the costs of poor quality are traditionally picked up by the accounting department. Even this small percentage amounts to 5% to 10% of sales—a huge waste. My own studies of companies that have not entered the quality/customer revolution show that, for these companies, the cost of poor quality is an amazing *$100 to $200 per employee, per day!*

But the more insidious costs are those that conventional accounting—which, incidentally, still functions in the nineteenth century—has not been able to gather. Amounting to 80% of the costs of poor quality, they can account for a whopping 20% to 40% of sales!

Cycle time is the other half of the quality coin. It can be defined as the actual clock time from the start of a process—either a manufacturing, business, design, or service process—to its completion. The actual direct labor time for the process, known as theoretical cycle time, is only a small fraction (less than 10%) of this total cycle time. The rest is WASTE—waiting time, set-up time, transport time, storage time, inspection and test time, rework time, and approval time. It is important to assess the current cycle time for customer orders, new product introduction, manufacturing, and key business processes such as accounts receivable and accounts payable.

FIGURE 14: The Hidden Costs of Poor Quality

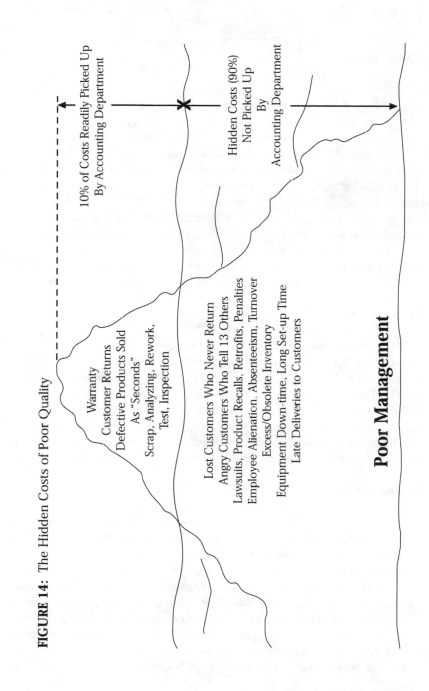

10% of Costs Readily Picked Up
By Accounting Department

Warranty
Customer Returns
Defective Products Sold
As "Seconds"
Scrap, Analyzing, Rework,
Test, Inspection

Hidden Costs (90%)
Not Picked Up
By
Accounting Department

Lost Customers Who Never Return
Angry Customers Who Tell 13 Others
Lawsuits, Product Recalls, Retrofits, Penalties
Employee Alienation, Absenteeism, Turnover
Excess/Obsolete Inventory
Equipment Down-time, Long Set-up Time
Late Deliveries to Customers

Poor Management

Management

Chapter 6 has detailed the salient features of a top management baseline: commitment and involvement; "walking the talk"; superordinate values; rewarding behaviors that reinforce customer service; and demonstrating customer commitment by thought, word, and deed.

The cost of the lifetime loss of a defecting customer was quantified in Chapter 6. What about the cost of poor quality/poor customer loyalty that is traceable to *poor management?* It is estimated that the very best CEOs make the right decisions about 70% of the time, with the average CEO falling below the 50% mark. What is the cost of these poor decisions in terms of customers, resources, structure, systems, and people? Between these two elements alone—lost customers and poor management—it is a wonder that so many companies are still in business. It's probably because the competition may be even worse!

People

This is a major assessment category. In the final analysis, service is a relationship between employees and customers. If a company devalues its employees, that is the message employees will pass on to its customers. People cannot be treated as pairs of hands. They cannot give of their best in a climate of fear, of lack of trust. They must be listened to, supported, encouraged, trained, and given opportunities to grow into their full potential. And true empowerment means giving them a piece of the action—administrative, managerial, and financial.

Organization

In the best tradition of business process reengineering, a company should evaluate whether it is moving away from bureaucracy, with its organizational charts and neat little boxes of cubby-hole departments, toward cross-functional teams, such as customer development, new product development, supply management, customer ordering, and the like. It should also assess whether it has a top corporate customer loyalty steering committee to guide the company's customer orientation; whether it has a "customer czar," or CCO (chief customer officer), in its ranks as the customer focal point; and whether the internal customer has been elevated to a position of importance, with the internal customer as the scorekeeper and the evaluator of the internal supplier's performance.

System

The assessment in this category should focus on whether policies and procedures exist for the good of the customer or for allowing management to command and control. It should also examine whether the old practices in hiring, training, evaluations, merit raises, and promotions have been revolutionized in order to change the behavior and values of employees and move to a customer-focused culture.

Tools

Traditionally, tools have been a weak link in most companies and in many disciplines. Using tools such as market research and mail surveys alone—coupled with a fixation on features (which leads to feature "creep") and on technological breakthroughs, and an overemphasis on quality for the sake of quality—is not very effective. Using these instruments distracts from the use of more powerful tools, such as quality function deployment, conjoint analysis, value engineering, design of experiments, and benchmarking. Knowledgeable implementation of these tools is essential in order to build up from a baseline level.

Design

The design of products and services should start with listening to the voice of the customer, not the voice of the design engineer or the voice of management. In addition, the assessment in this category should include the extent to which there are design processes to achieve zero variation (beyond zero defects) or zero field failures, minimal field service, built-in diagnostics and ergonomics, low costs, and short cycle time.

Suppliers

Just as we cannot have happy customers without happy, productive employees, we cannot have happy customers without key suppliers who are encouraged to establish partnerships with a company along the same lines that the company builds with its core customers. The baseline audit should assess the same adherence to partnership principles as is done with customers, and it should include the amount and quality of active, concrete help rendered by and to each side.

Manufacturing

From a customer's perspective, there are two major elements associated with the effectiveness of manufacturing: quality and cycle time. In the last 10 years, manufacturing quality has received a great deal of attention and has experienced an appreciable amount of improvement. Focusing on cycle time is a much newer approach, but with pull systems and just-in-time practices (that have replaced old MRP-2 systems), delinquencies in delivery to the customer have fallen by factors of 10:1.

Field Operations

This is where the rubber meets the road—where the customer is able to observe the company's products and services firsthand. Baseline assessments should include packing and transportation, installation and operating instructions, and the accuracy, completeness, and timing of repair service.

Support Services

As product quality has steadily improved, customer dissatisfactions are increasingly centered on poor support service—billing errors, wrong destinations, a runaround on inquiries, unsatisfactory problem resolution, and—worse—lack of attention.

Step 2: Internal Benchmarking—A Baseline	Rating				
	1	2	3	4	5
A. Measurement					
1. The number of defecting customers as a percentage of the total number of customers is less than 5%.					
2. The longevity of core customers retained is measured in years.					
3. The value added for each core customer is measured by core customers themselves.					
4. The cost of poor quality, as measured by the accounting department, is analyzed and reduced.					
5. The hidden costs of poor quality are being quantified.					
6. The cycle times of key processes—manufacturing, design, business—are being measured and systematically reduced.					
B. Management (see audit in Chapter 6)					
C. People					
1. There is a climate of full trust between management and employees.					
2. Employees are not afraid to speak out, generate ideas, and even constructively criticize management.					
3. Employees are given regular feedback on their performance, especially as their activities impact customers.					
4. Employees are given increasing responsibility in administering and managing their work areas.					

Step 2: Internal Benchmarking—A Baseline (cont'd)	Rating				
	1	2	3	4	5
5. Employees are given financial incentives based on their performance; employees perceive that they have "a piece of the action" and a stake in the success of the company.					
6. Customer-contact employees are given discretion to use any means to win over dissatisfied customers, including financial compensation within limits.					
D. Organization					
1. The organization chart is de-emphasized to prevent a vertical silo mentality and turf wars; the team concept—especially cross-functional teams—is encouraged and nurtured.					
2. A top management customer loyalty steering committee is established to guide and monitor complete alignment with the customer.					
3. A top management person is designated as the customer's advocate, either as an ombudsman or as the chief customer officer (CCO).					
4. The internal customer is elevated to a scorekeeper and evaluator of an internal supplier. Performance appraisals are determined more by the internal customer and less by the supervisor.					
E. System					
1. Policies and procedures of little or no consequence to the customer are de-emphasized or eliminated.					
2. The hiring of employees includes tests for the candidate's potential as a team player and for customer sensitivity.					

Step 2: Internal Benchmarking—A Baseline (cont'd)	Rating				
	1	2	3	4	5
3. Employee evaluations are based on team (rather than individual) performance.					
4. Small, automatic, and annual merit raises are discarded in favor of more substantial bonuses, based upon value added to the customer and fulfillment of goals.					
5. Promotions are based on ability and potential for growth, rather than just on performance.					
F. Tools					
1. Quality function deployment, conjoint analysis, value research, and allied tools are regularly used to capture the "voice of the customer."					
2. Design of Experiments (DOE)[1] is used to translate customer requirements into engineering specifications and tolerances and to parts specifications and tolerances for suppliers.					
3. Multiple environment overstress tests[2] (MEOST) are used to ensure that field reliability for customers moves toward zero field failures.					
4. Value engineering[3] is used to reduce costs to customers and simultaneously add value to customers—as perceived by them.					
5. Benchmarking[4] is used to close the gap between the company and a best-in-class company in terms of a product, technique, function, or department.					
6. Total productive maintenance[5] is used to improve process yields, up-time, and efficiency.					

Step 2: Internal Benchmarking—A Baseline (cont'd)	Rating				
	1	2	3	4	5
G. Design					
1. Customers are systematically consulted before the start of a design to determine their most important needs and requirements; they are asked to compare the company against its best competitor on each requirement.					
2. Reverse engineering or competitive analysis is used to compare the company's design versus its best competitor's in terms of features, materials, manufacturing, reliability, and cost.					
3. Techniques to achieve zero variation[6], such as the design of experiments, are used at the prototype stage of design.					
4. Techniques to achieve zero field failures[7], such as multiple environment overstress tests, are used at the prototype stage of design.					
5. Designs for manufacturability methods[8] are systematically employed to simplify manufacturing the designs and to quantify their manufacturability.					
6. Built-in diagnostics are designed to facilitate ease of repair, preferably by the customer directly.					
7. Ergonomics are considered in making the product or service user-friendly.					
8. Product/service liability prevention techniques[9] are employed to prevent danger to the customer and minimize related lawsuits.					
9. Cycle time reduction techniques are used to design the product/service in a fraction of the time used for older designs.					

Step 2: Internal Benchmarking—A Baseline (cont'd)	Rating				
	1	2	3	4	5
10. Cost targeting, group technology, and value engineering techniques are used.					
11. Concurrent engineering is used to employ a cross-functional team approach during the entire design cycle.					
H. Suppliers[10]					
1. A win-win partnership is established with key suppliers as a key corporate strategy.					
2. This partnership is sustained with uncompromising ethics and full trust on both sides.					
3. Active, concrete, and mutual help is rendered by both the company and its partnership suppliers for their mutual benefit.					
4. A continuous price reduction for the company is targeted along with an increased profitability for partnership suppliers.					
I. Manufacturing					
1. Key process parameters are characterized and optimized, using design of experiments, to achieve a minimum Cp of 2.0 (*Cp* is defined as the specification width divided by the process width of a given parameter).					
2. Key process parameters are "frozen," with positrol,[11] to ensure that optimized parameters stay within their predetermined limits.					
3. Key quality peripherals, such as metrology, environments, configuration control, and change control are kept under tight control, using process certification.[12]					

Step 2: Internal Benchmarking—A Baseline (cont'd)	Rating				
	1	2	3	4	5
4. Operator-controllable errors are prevented using poka-yoke[13] methods.					
5. Cycle time reduction is used to move manufacturing toward pull systems, focused factories, total preventive maintenance (TPM), small lots, reduced set-up times, and dedicated equipment and people.					
J. Field Operations					
1. Packing and transportation practices are reviewed to make sure that the customer receives the product with no damage or delay.					
2. Installation and operating instructions are made understandable and user-friendly.					
3. Customer understanding of applying the company's product or service is achieved through training, video tapes, seminars, and personal visits by competent technical people.					
4. Feedback is sought from the customer on the accuracy, completeness, and timing of repair service.					
K. Support Services					
1. Business process improvements[14] are the norm, utilizing cross-functional teams, flow charts, mapping, and "out-of-box" thinking.					
2. The "next operation as customer"[15] is firmly established, whereby the internal customer— rather than the boss—evaluates an internal supplier (individual or team).					

Step 2: Internal Benchmarking—A Baseline (cont'd)	Rating				
	1	2	3	4	5
3. Nonproduct customer issues, such as billing errors, accounts receivable, access to key supplier personnel, and speedy resolution of complaints or concerns are courteously, promptly, and completely addressed.					
4. Attention to customers and their needs is paid long after sales.					

Notes

1. Keki R. Bhote, *World Class Quality—Using Design of Experiments to Make it Happen*, American Management Association, 1991.
2. Keki R. Bhote, *Strategic Supply Management*, American Management Association, 1989.
3. Larry Miles, *Value Analysis Techniques*, McGraw-Hill, 1982.
4. Michael Spendolini, *The Benchmarking Book*, American Management Association, 1992.
5. Seiichi Nakajima, *Total Productive Maintenance*, Productivity Press, 1988.
6. Bhote, *World Class Quality*.
7. Bhote, *Strategic Supply Management*.
8. Jeffrey Boothroyd and Peter Dewhurst, *Product Design for Manufacturing and Assembly*, Boothroyd & Dewhurst, Inc., 1987.
9. Bhote, *Strategic Supply Management*.
10. Ibid.
11. Bhote, *World Class Quality*.
12. Ibid.
13. Shigeo Shingo, *Zero Q.C. Source Inspection and Poka Yoke*, Productivity Press, 1985.
14. Keki R. Bhote, *Next Operation As Customer*, American Management Association Briefing, 1991.
15. Bhote, *Next Operation As Customer*.

8

Step 3: Determining Customer Requirements

"You may have the best dog food in the world, but if the dogs don't eat it. . . ."

—A Motorola saying

From the Voice of the Engineer to the Voice of the Customer

This chapter focuses on the several methods of determining customer requirements. Until a decade ago, the prevalent practice for product managers and engineers was gazing into a crystal ball to figure out what the customers wanted. The trouble was that the crystal ball was murky. Even worse, management and their engineers, in their arrogance, believed that they knew more about what their customers wanted than the customers knew themselves. The result? Approximately 80% of new products launched failed in the marketplace.

Market Research—Another Cloudy Crystal Ball

In their attempt to graduate from products developed in isolation and thrust down the customer's throat with slick advertising, many companies turned to market research as the answer. Often, however, this turned out to be quantitative research—demographics that amounted to little more than mere head counting. Such research might ask, "How did you hear about us?" and other peripheral questions. But it does not ask, "What major experiences influenced your decision to try our product or service?" It does not research why a customer has defected. Further, it is often done in isolation by sales-oriented personnel who lack depth in such disciplines as *quality, product design,* and *service.* It is not a team exercise.

Market research's most memorable faux pas include the Edsel car, a product based on a stupendous piece of market research that ended in Ford Motor Company's worst launch fiasco. Or consider the more recent case of Dove—the ice cream bar—which was panned by market research, but which achieved a meteoric success.

Powerful Tools for Determining Customer Requirements

Fortunately, much better methods for taking the pulse of customer requirements have been developed over the last 20 years. Space permits only a brief description of each method. (For a detailed explanation of value research, sensitivity analysis, and multi-attribute evaluation, see K. Bhote, *Strategic Supply Management,* American Management Association, 1989.)

Value research. A core group of potential customers who represent the center of gravity of the larger customer population is given a product to evaluate. They keep track of their experiences and report back their strong "dislikes," their strong "likes," and their "neutrals" (features about which they are indifferent). The company then corrects the strong "dislikes," advertises and promotes the strong "likes," and applies value engineering to the unimportant features to reduce costs. Value research, while simple in concept, is powerful in its effectiveness.

Customer window model. This is a plot of product features and customer requirements with two axes. The first axis ranges from what the customer "gets" to "does not get." The second axis ranges from what the customer "wants" to "does not want." This produces a "window" with four quadrants, as shown in FIGURE 15. A concentration of the company's features in the lower right quadrant is overkill—a waste. A concentration in the upper left is a danger signal. A concentration in the upper right quadrant is the ideal.

FIGURE 16 shows a variation of the customer window model, using information from customer interviews for a consumer nondurables company. It provides a concise presentation of not only a customer's evaluation of various aspects of a supplier's performance, but also

FIGURE 15: The Customer Window Model

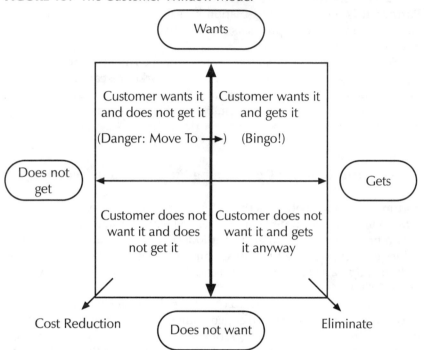

the apparent "disconnect" between the customer's important requirements and the emphasis placed by the supplier's management. The
supplier performed poorly on items important to the customer, while
the supplier's management emphasized requirements that were not
very important to the customer.

   Sensitivity analysis. This is another simple but powerful tool that
most companies have not exploited. The tool allows management, in
cooperation with core customers, to examine the level of each feature
or requirement compared with its cost. If the gain in level is large for
a relatively small increase in price, it would result in a mutual "go"
decision. If, on the other hand, the gain in level is small for a large
increase in cost and price, it would be a "no go." Similarly, if a decrease in the level of a feature or requirement is small relative to a large
decrease in cost and price, it would be a "go" decision. If vice versa, it
would be a "no go."

FIGURE 16: A "Disconnect" Between a Customer's Importance of Various Requirements and Its Supplier's Emphasis

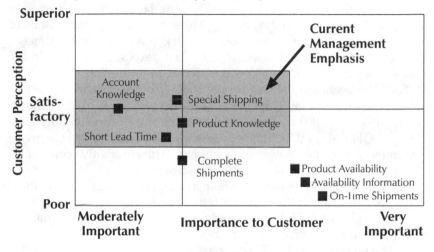

Multi-attribute evaluation. This is a matrix in which the horizontal leg lists the product's various features—as determined by the customer—and the vertical leg lists companies that offer that product and features (including your own company and its best competitors). Each feature is given an importance scale, say, from 1 to 5. Each company is then rated by customers for each feature, also on a scale such as 1 to 5. The weighted rating in each box is the product of the importance of the feature multiplied by the company rating. The weighted ratings are then added horizontally to determine which is the best company, overall. Each feature is also scrutinized vertically to see how a company compares with its competition.

Conjoint analysis. This is a tool that combines several features and presents them to potential customers or focus groups as a single option. There are other options, also, each combining alternative levels of each of the desired features. The customers can then choose among options, but they cannot cherry-pick a feature level in another option. Conjoint analysis has the advantage of segmenting customers according to variations in tastes and varying budgets. It also has the advantage of helping the manufacturer focus on a limited number of models and thus achieve greater standardization.

As an example, in the days when consumers could choose a wide variety of features in the cars they purchased, the permutations were endless. There could be 64,000 versions of the Ford LTD model—with no car exactly like another! By contrast, the Honda Accord had only 400 possible versions. Today, the Big Three have learned the lessons of combining options for greater commonality, if not standardization.

Quality function deployment (QFD). First developed in Japan in the Kobe shipyards in 1970, QFD was introduced to the West in the mid-1980s. This technique is thoroughly defined in Yoji Akao's excellent book, *Quality Function Deployment* (Productivity Press, 1988). Today, there are over 10,000 companies in America and Europe that are dabbling in QFD—I say dabbling because they have not achieved the greatest mileage from this powerful technique. (The automotive companies are probably the furthest along in implementing QFD.) If done right, quality function deployment can help a company design and manufacture products in half the time, with half the manpower, with half the defects, and with half the costs *and*—at the same time—best quantify and prioritize customer requirements.

The objectives of a QFD study are to:

- ascertain and prioritize customer requirements before a new design begins—in other words, capture the voice of the customer rather than the voice of the engineer;
- obtain the customer's view of the company's strengths and weaknesses as compared with its competitor's on each customer requirement;
- compare the company's strengths and weaknesses with its competitor's on each engineering specification—through reverse engineering (i.e., competitive analysis);
- highlight incompatibilities in design (negative correlations); and, as a bottom line,
- pinpoint the important, the new, and the difficult in the preliminary design.

At first glance, the "House of Quality" matrix that results from QFD appears to be complicated, but with an hour or two of coaching, it can easily be demystified. FIGURE 17 shows a QFD analysis of computer printer paper. The two left columns indicate customer requirements (the what) and the importance of each requirement. The vertical columns on top translate these customer requirements into engineering specifications (the how). The middle section is a relationship matrix that quantifies the strength of the relationship between each customer requirement and its corresponding engineering specification. The right column compares the customer's rating of the company, for each requirement, against the competition. The lower portions of the House of Quality indicate the target value of each engineering specification and how well they compare (see the technical evaluation part of FIGURE 17) to the competition's specifications. The roof of the house shows how well each engineering specification is positively or negatively correlated to other specifications.

Most QFD studies, however, are poorly constructed, interpreted, and implemented. Some of the more common pitfalls include:

• No extension is made beyond the first "what"—customer requirements—and the first "how"—engineering specifications. This is only the first cascade. Effective QFD requires several cascades of the "what" and "how," from engineering specifications which become the new "what" to parts specifications, the new "how." Further cascadings go from parts specifications to process specifications to test specifications, etc. But, even in Japan, 90% of the companies using QFD rarely go beyond the first cascade. As a result, the full benefits of QFD—of tying these important processes together into a unified whole—are not realized.

• Most QFD studies, even for the first cascade, concentrate only on performance parameters and ignore the other vital elements of customer enthusiasm (refer to FIGURE 11). Some of these ignored elements may be far more important to the customer than performance characteristics.

• QFD practitioners usually list too many customer requirements, making the practice so complex that companies sometimes tend to throw the baby out with the bathwater.

Fathoming the Customer's Mind

But even with QFD as a powerful tool, the question remains: How do you really fathom what is in customers' minds—their needs, their expectations, their requirements? There are many techniques; a few are effective, but most are marginal. The latter include listening for constructive or critical comments at trade shows; making observations at

FIGURE 17: Quality Function Deployment: "The House of Quality"

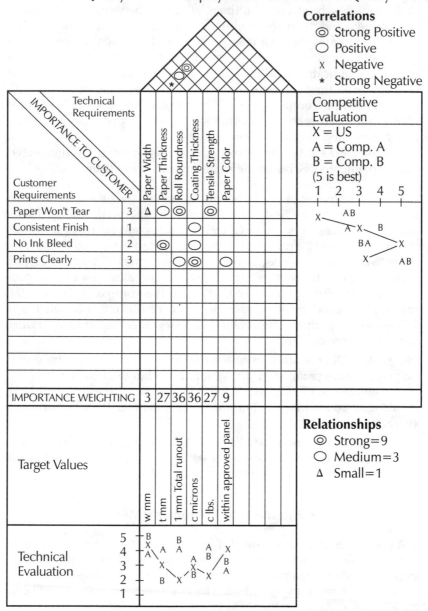

customer sites, distributorships, dealerships, and service centers; setting up 800 numbers so that customers can call in toll-free; mailing "quickie" cards to customers who have used or bought the product and soliciting their comments at the first point of usage; using mail surveys; and implementing "hidden" surveys (i.e., surveys that withhold the name of the sponsoring company, generally conducted through an intermediary such as a consultant). These methods do generate some information about customer requirements, but it is—for the most part—filtered information obtained through indirect contact with customers. With some of the above techniques, it is also too late. The product or service is already in the customers' hands.

However, there are three techniques that are highly effective.

1. *Focus groups, clinics, panels.* The company assembles typical persons, representing the center of gravity of the projected customer population, and solicits their opinions and recommendations on "clay models" or prototypes of the product or service being launched. The discussions are led by a trained facilitator or are observed by key company personnel behind a one-way glass panel. The advantages here include instant feedback, as well as a determination of consensus or diversity of opinions. The disadvantage is that a "herd mentality" may develop: A dominant person may pull the rest of the panel into a forced agreement, or the panel members may be hesitant to speak their minds.

2. *Customer-contact personnel inputs.* Employees who frequently come into contact with customers can be a very good source of information. Even though this source is best utilized after the product or service is in the field, the inputs, ideas, and recommendations of customer-contact employees can be most useful on older products or services as they may impact newer products or services.

3. *One-on-one in-depth interviews.* In the final analysis, none of the above techniques is as effective as spending time with customers themselves, one-on-one, in their own environment. This may be time-consuming and costly to do for the whole consuming public, but it is strongly recommended for those core customers who constitute only 20% of the total customer population yet make up 80% of total sales volume.

Interviews should be conducted not only with people in a customer organization who make purchasing decisions but with actual users who "feel the product, smell the product, deal in the product."

Most face-to-face interviews should last one to one-and-a-half hours. The interviewer should let the customer describe—without structure or prompting at first—the key product or service attributes that would lead to an increase or decline in purchases. In some cases, managers from the company may conduct the interviews. For others, outside support may be preferable, using "blind" interviewers, not identified with a specific company, in order to get unbiased responses.

Interviews generally continue until key responses are consistently repeated and until unique responses describe exceptional or unusual customers' responses. This is likely to happen after about 12 to 15 interviews.

From Mass Marketing to Mass Customization

A few years ago, mass production was replaced among progressive companies with lean production. Instead of the old economy of scale, big runs, and large economic build quantities (EBQs)—where holding costs were balanced against production costs—lean production engendered innovations where an EBQ of 1 could become almost as efficient as EBQs of 1,000 or 100,000.

There is a similar innovation in the world of customers and their requirements—a movement away from mass marketing to mass customization. Mass marketing means pushing a large variety of options into the marketplace and hoping that each option will generate a sufficient number of customers to make the production of each option cost effective. Such a practice results in a tyranny of choices that customers really do not want. The mass marketeer generates a list of the most likely prospective customers and solicits them with messages that the marketeer tries to customize by *guessing* their tastes. Mass customization, by contrast, means conducting a dialogue with each core customer—one at a time—and using the increasingly more relevant and detailed feedback to produce the best products or services for that customer. *This binds producer and consumer together in an interactive, learning relationship.* (See Pine, Peppers, and Rogers, "Do You Want to Keep Your Customers Forever?", *Harvard Business Review*, March-April 1995.)

This interactive learning relationship means that the more customers teach the company, the better it will become at providing exactly what they want, how they want it, where they want it, and when they want it; the more difficult it will be for a competitor to lure them away; and the easier it will be for the company to maintain customer loyalty and retention for a long, long time. Mass customization and learning relationships would not have been possible without revolutions in information technology and flexible manufacturing systems (FMS), which enable companies to gather and store vast amounts of data on the needs and preferences of individual core customers and to customize large volumes of goods and services for them at a relatively low cost.

Mass marketing is both costly and environmentally hostile. Consider the daily newspaper. It weighs 55% more today than it did ten years ago. There are supplements, such as the suburban, metro, business, sports, fashion, auto, and home sections, as well as advertisements. Between 70% and 80% of the newspaper is immediately thrown out by most people without being read! But if newspaper publishers could interact with their loyal, repetitive customers on a periodic basis and determine what such customers really wanted, costs to both could be reduced and paper pollution cut by at least 50%. There could be the renaissance of a "green" revolution!

Another example is the grocery store. According to *Product News,* the number of new products introduced each year increased from fewer than 3,000 in 1980 to more than 10,000 in 1988 and to more than 17,000 in 1993. *Progressive Grocer* reports that the number of stock-keeping units in the average supermarket doubled to more than 30,000 from 1980 to 1994.

How can mass customizing be introduced? As mentioned in Chapter 4, Reichheld and Sasser tackle this problem in "Zero Defections: Quality Comes to Services" (*Harvard Business Review,* September-October 1990). Further, Pine, Peppers, and Rogers (cited above) outline the example of Peapod, a grocery shopping and delivery service based in Evanston, Illinois. Its core customers buy a software application for $29.95 that enables them to access Peapod's database. Peapod's office is linked to the mainframe databases of the supermarkets at which it shops on behalf of its customers. Using personal computers, customers can request a list of items by category, by item, by brand, by what is on sale in the store on a given day—or even by the latest popular classification, nutritional value.

Peapod charges its customers $4.95 per month for the service and a per-order charge of $5.00 plus 5% of the order amount. But despite such charges, customers save money because they do better comparison shopping, use more coupons, and make fewer impulse buys than they would in a real supermarket—and the time savings is the frosting on the cake.

Peapod uses every customer interaction as an opportunity to learn. For each transaction, it asks the customer, "How did we do on your last order?" Peapod gets a response of at least 35%, compared with other general customer satisfaction surveys that get an average response of less than 10%. Peapod is in tune with its customers—and it shows. It has instituted a variety of changes and options, such as faster deliveries, nutritional data, and instructions on where to leave deliveries when customers are not at home.

Peapod has to be efficient, despite the rates it charges in this low-margin business. It mass-customizes all shopping and delivery processes. Each order is filled by a generalist who shops the store's aisles and pays for the groceries, often at special Peapod counters. At each stage—ordering, shopping, holding, and delivery—the processes are modularized to provide personalized service at low cost. The results? Peapod's four-year-old service has 7,500 customers and their customer retention rate is greater than 80%. And the service accounts for an average of 15% of the sales volume at the 12 Jewel and Safeway stores where Peapod shops for its customers.

If You Do Not Learn from Past Mistakes, You Are Likely to Repeat Them

The great majority of companies display a fundamental weakness in their determination of customer requirements: They concentrate only on existing customers or on new ones. They do not poll former customers or noncustomers. Former customers can provide a wealth of information about why they became disenchanted with the company. Likewise, non-customers—although harder to identify—can stipulate the reasons why they were never enticed to try the company's products or services. A concerted effort should be made, using the highly effective one-on-one interview technique where possible, to touch these two important bases. Former customers should not be looked upon as "history." Mistakes of the past that resulted in losing them should be turned into preventive action for the future. Defections management, detailed in Chapter 12, is the way to plug this hole in the dike.

Step 3: Determining Customer Requirements	Rating				
	1	2	3	4	5
A. Poor Methods that Should Not Be Used for Determining Customer Requirements					
1. Management and engineering listen to the "voice of the customer" and do not assume that they know customer requirements better than the customer does.					
2. Slick and false advertising, used to lure unwary customers, is forbidden.					
3. Market research is used only peripherally to determine customer demographics, not as a sure-fire way of determining customer requirements.					
B. Modern Techniques to Gauge the Pulse of Customer Requirements					
1. One or more of the following methods are used to determine customer requirements: value research; window model; sensitivity analysis; multi-attribute evaluation; conjoint analysis.					
2. The use of quality function deployment (QFD) is encouraged as one of the best ways to determine the "voice of the customer."					
3. The second and third cascades of QFD are also employed to translate engineering specifications into parts, process, and test specifications.					
C. Probing the Customers' Minds to Determine Needs and Expectations					
1. Focus groups, clinics, and panels are used for feedback on models and prototypes.					
2. Customer-contact employees' inputs, ideas, and recommendations are systematically sought.					

Step 3: Determining Customer Requirements (cont'd)	Rating				
	1	2	3	4	5
3. One-on-one, in-depth interviews are conducted with core customers as the best and most systematic way of determining customer needs, requirements, and expectations.					
4. Mass customization is employed when interacting with each core customer in order to produce the best product or service for that customer.					
5. The company combines information technology with flexible manufacturing systems (FMS) to produce low-cost products and services for its individualized customers.					
6. Former customers' and noncustomers' inputs are eagerly sought to round out the perspective given by the techniques listed above.					

9

Step 4: Assessing the Capabilities of the Competition

"If you know your enemy and know yourself, you
need not fear the result of a hundred battles."

—Sun Tsu, Chinese general, 500 B.C.

Measuring Competition's Pulse

Chapter 7, on internal benchmarking, began with the premise, "Know
yourself before you know your competition." It detailed a roadmap
by which a company can assess how well it is positioned to serve its
customers.

This chapter follows Sun Tsu's advice to "know your enemy."
In modern terms, that means "know your competition." This chapter
details a number of techniques by which the capabilities of the company's best competitor can be assessed and the gap between the two
companies—in terms of customer satisfaction and loyalty—can be
quantified.

1. Quality Function Deployment (QFD)

Recall, for a moment, the description of quality function deployment
presented in Chapter 8. In the "House of Quality" matrix—QFD's sig-

nature—the right side is devoted to a rating *done by the customer* of how a company compares against two of its best competitors on each of the customer's important requirements. The usual scale is 1 to 5, with 1 being the worst and 5 the best. (Some companies go further and superimpose a target and a management "override" factor to further quantify this competitive assessment.)

The bottom portion of the QFD matrix is another assessment of the same two competitors, but this time performed by the company. This reverse engineering, or competitive evaluation, process compares how each engineering parameter of the company (the "how" in the matrix) is rated—on a scale of 1 to 5—against these best competitors.

As a result of these comprehensive evaluations, the company has a much clearer and more quantitative comparison of its strengths and weaknesses, compared with its competitors'.

2. Benchmarking

Ever since benchmarking was introduced to the Western world by Xerox, it has become a powerful tool for improvement in any corporation. Besides internal benchmarking, there are two other types of benchmarking that should be pursued. The first is competitive benchmarking—determining who is the best competitor. The second is generic benchmarking—determining which is the best company in the field. In this case, a noncompetitor may be even better than a competitor.

Applied to the discipline of customer service, both types of benchmarking processes are in order. Competitive benchmarking has an advantage in that the company's performance can be directly compared between two companies with similar products, services, and customers. It has a disadvantage in that the competitor benchmark company may not cooperate in the study and could regard its customer service information as highly proprietary. Generic benchmarking has the advantage of much easier access to and cooperation by the benchmark company since it is not a competitor.

Time permitting, both types of benchmarking should be pursued so that the company gets two perspectives on best practices associated with customer service.

3. Industry Reports

Another important source of competitive performance is the variety of reports published in the media:

- The J. D. Powers reports on customer satisfaction with cars are well-known, widely read, and authentic. They are taken very seriously by the automotive companies, who seldom fail to use them in their advertising—when favorable. J. D. Powers also performs comparative evaluations of companies in several other businesses.
- Government reports compare airlines on accident rates, on-time arrivals, and lost baggage.
- Consumer magazines rate various products made by companies and are frequently consulted by customers in their buying decisions. But there can be nagging questions about slants in the questionnaires, sample sizes, evaluation techniques, and data shading.
- Commissioned studies are made on a wide variety of products, companies, universities, hospitals, etc., rating them annually.

4. Independent Laboratories

Independent laboratories are often used by companies to perform product evaluations. Most of these render above-board service, but there is always the danger that the one who pays the piper gets to call the tune!

Graphical Portrayal of Company vs. Competitive Performance on Key Customer Requirements

Sometimes, core customers present a comparison of their rating of a company with its best competitor on each important customer requirement using a graph or chart. FIGURE 18 depicts such a chart, where a large original equipment manufacturer rated a supplier that provided engineers to this company on a contract basis. It also rated a competitive supplier.

The importance (to the customer) and the rating (by the customer) scales are from 1 to 5, with 1 being the worst and 5 being the best. Given that 2.5 is the minimum acceptable importance and rating, FIG-URE 18 shows that both the company and its competitor are not in the lower left (danger) quadrant; both have four of the seven customer requirements in the top right (ideal) quadrant. The company is superior to its competitor in two requirements that are very important to the customer—placement speed and placement professionalism. But the company's high costs need to be reduced and its reputation, in the eyes of the customer, improved.

A graphical portrayal is a visual integration of (1) the importance that a customer attaches to its requirements, and (2) the strengths and weaknesses of a supplier vis-a-vis its best competitor.

Step 4: Analyzing the Capabilities of the Competition	Rating				
	1	2	3	4	5
1. Quality function deployment (QFD) is systematically used, whereby the core customers rate the company against its best competitors on each important customer requirement.					
2. The company performs reverse engineering on its competitor's products or services and compares each of its engineering specifications against its competitor's and against a target value for that specification.					
3. The company benchmarks its customer service process against its best competitor's.					
4. The company benchmarks its customer service process against noncompeting companies that have the best reputations for such service.					
5. The company utilizes a variety of industry reports to compare its products and services to the competition's.					
6. The company utilizes independent laboratories and/or outside consultants to compare its products and services to the competition's.					

FIGURE 18: Customer Rating of Company vs. Competitor on Its Important Requirements

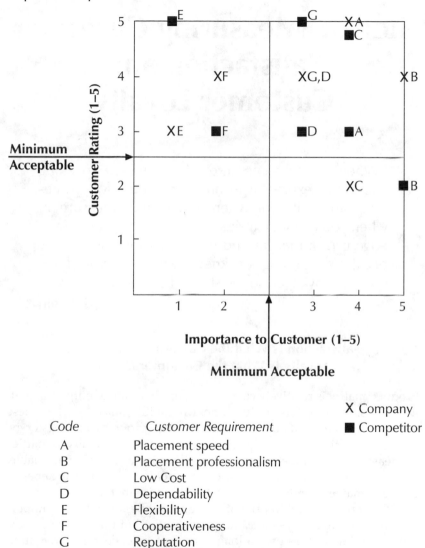

Code	Customer Requirement
A	Placement speed
B	Placement professionalism
C	Low Cost
D	Dependability
E	Flexibility
F	Cooperativeness
G	Reputation

10

Step 5: Measuring Customer Satisfaction and Customer Loyalty

"When you can measure what you are speaking about and express it in numbers, you know something about it; but when you cannot measure it, when you cannot express it in numbers, your knowledge is of a meager and unsatisfactory kind. It may be the beginning of knowledge, but you have scarcely advanced to the stage of science."

—Lord Kelvin

Satisfaction Is What the Customer SAYS (It Is); Loyalty Is What the Customer DOES

Product quality is relatively easy to measure in terms of outgoing quality, yields, total defects per unit, field reliability, and the like. These are objective, quantifiable parameters, and progress can easily be tracked over time. Except for field repairs, service quality is harder to measure. Its parameters are more subjective and less quantifiable. Customer satisfaction is even harder to measure, because it depends on the human element: Customer satisfaction is what the customer *says* it is. Customer loyalty, on the other hand, while far, far more important, is—paradoxically—*easier* to quantify. For both a relatively short time period as well as over a long period of time, customer retention and its reciprocal, customer defections, are eminently quantifiable. Customers vote—either for or against companies—with their feet and with their pocketbooks.

This chapter deals with the principal modes of customer feedback and the various customer satisfaction and customer loyalty metrics.

The Survey Questionnaire

The preamble to successful customer feedback is designing a comprehensive survey questionnaire. A poorly designed questionnaire is often the cause of serious "disconnects" between a company and its customers.

Questionnaire Design—Do's and Don'ts

1. Start with a pilot questionnaire, with pilot customers, to fine-tune the questionnaire into its final form.
2. State the objective of the questionnaire in simple, clear, nondemanding terms.
3. Keep the questionnaire short (fewer than 25 questions, preferably), easy to fill out, and user-friendly. The surveyed customers should never be asked to spend more than 20 minutes of their valuable time.
4. Make sure that the questionnaire is neutrally worded and that there are no company management biases or slants in the questions.
5. Let the customers, *not management*, select the parameters that are important to them. One major health insurer, for example, felt that speed in answering queries and accuracy were the important parameters. As it turned out, however, what many customers wanted most was clarity of explanations and reassurance that their problems would be resolved.
6. Select parameters (no more than 10 to 15) that reflect those elements of customer satisfaction *that are the most important to customers*. Use the results of a QFD study to determine importance ranking. The more parameters there are, the greater the customer's dilemma in rating each of them and the more difficult the analysis. For example, American Express uses 180 parameters to measure customer satisfaction. That's overkill; it is also expensive and ineffective. It can cause you to lose sight of the forest for the trees.

On the opposite side of the spectrum, companies like Caterpillar, Auto Spark, and Kroger (for its suppliers) concentrate on just one parameter—speed of delivery. Caterpillar prides itself on being able to dispatch a service part to any location in the world within 48 hours. Auto Spark, with an inventory of 30,000 parts, can deliver a part to a customer anywhere in the United States in one day.

7. Include important questions such as:

- *Would you buy this product or service again from our company?*
- *Would you buy a product of the same brand name (i.e., other products made by the company)?*
- *Would you recommend this product (or service) to a friend?*
- *How do you view similar products or services from our competitors?*
- *How can we better serve you?*

8. In service companies, use a flowchart—starting with the customer's first contact with the company and ending with the last—to frame sequential questions. As an example, a questionnaire about a hotel's services could start with advance reservations, then ask about the parking services, registration process, room comfort, food quality, health club facilities, and so on, and end with a rating of the check-out process.

9. Request that customers state *how long* they have been the company's customers; *how often* they have used the company's products or services in that time; whether they have switched to the company's competitor; and whether they have had positive or negative experiences with the competitor.

10. Leave room for comments.

11. Leave space for customers to write their names and phone numbers, but make this optional.

12. Use professionals with a proven track record (either within the company or outside consultants) to design the questionnaire.

13. In telephone or person-to-person or group surveys, use trained interviewers who are sensitive to customers—their moods, their frustrations, and their enthusiasm.

14. When possible, use outsiders as interviewers. Customers are more frank with them than with a company interviewer.

15. End with a sincere "thank you" for imposing on the customer's time, and express your commitment to follow up on the responses to improve your service.
16. Find ways to motivate people to complete the survey, including incentives—financial or otherwise—where appropriate.

Determination of the Customer Sample for Surveys

There are several principles of sampling theory that should be adhered to:

- The *absolute size* of the sample is more important than *sample size as a percentage* of the total customer population.
- Segmentation, by customer type, is essential (e.g., OEMs vs. end-users; distributors/dealers vs. end-users; core customers vs. others; their geographic location; and gender, age, etc.).
- When customers are asked to record their experiences with a company's product or service, a sample size of 30 for each customer segment is sufficient, provided the center of gravity of the customer population has been identified. (Beyond the "magic number" of 30 for sample size for each segmentation, the responses tend to be repetitive; this adds costs and has no additional informative value.)
- Within each segmented sample, customer selections should be randomized. Competitors' customers should also be sampled as a separate segment.

Frequency of Polling

The number of times customers are surveyed for determining satisfaction varies with different products, services, and types of customers. During its monopoly days, AT&T was comfortable with an annual survey. Customers couldn't jump ship. But with a revolution raging in long-line communications and with the intensity of new competitors, including the Baby Bells, AT&T now polls its customers much more frequently. At the other extreme is Federal Express, which polls its customers once a month. Its volume of business and the number of steps in its delivery cycle warrant the more frequent polling. A general rule is once per quarter.

For core customers, however, the polling should be more or less continuous. Konusuke Matsushita, the renowned founder of the Matsushita empire, counseled his sales force to "take the customers' skin temperature every day." Core customers need close, constant attention. Their changing needs, requirements, and expectations must be carefully monitored and addressed. Information technology and mass customization are the high-tech vehicles to achieve this. But, in the final analysis, there is no substitute for a *live, personal* relationship between a company's representatives and its core customers. Service is more important than products; relationships are more important than service.

Principal Modes of Customer Feedback

This section outlines a series of customer feedback methods. Each method is given an effectiveness scale (the author's opinion) from 1 to 10, with 1 being the least and 10 the most effective.

1. *Mail surveys (Effectiveness: 2).* The advantages of mail surveys are that they are

- inexpensive, fast;
- able to cover a large customer base (even 100%);
- characterized by an economy of questions;
- good for a preliminary reading of the customer's pulse.

Their disadvantages are that

- the customer response rate is extremely poor (5% to 10%);
- they provide only one-way communication;
- they are cold and impersonal;
- the customer responses are biased toward those with complaints and against those who are satisfied and do not feel the need to reply.

2. *Telephone surveys (Effectiveness: 4).* The advantages of telephone surveys are that

- they are more cost effective than mail surveys, even though the expense outlay is higher;

- they can be tailored for specific objectives, complaints, or concerns;
- they provide two-way communication, allowing customers' emotional factors to be registered.

The disadvantages are that

- targeted customers are often difficult to reach;
- the public is inundated with telemarketing, especially computer-generated calls. This causes customers to hang up on genuine surveys.
- the all-important body language signals of face-to-face interviews are absent.

Telephone surveys should be conducted only by trained and experienced interviewers; cold calls, long interviews (over 20 minutes), and a long list of questions (more than 20) are the surest way to turn customers off.

3. *Focus groups, round tables, clinics, panels (Effectiveness: 7)*. The value of these groups in determining customer requirements has been discussed in Chapter 8. They have even greater value in measuring customer satisfaction. Their advantages and disadvantages have also been listed in Chapter 8, with the former by far outweighing the latter. Including former customers and noncustomers in focus groups is desirable, because they could give insights on the shortcomings of the company's products or services.

4. *Top management visits (Effectiveness: 8)*. The absolute necessity of top management visiting core customers was highlighted in Chapter 5. The best feedback comes not from top management talking to their CEO equivalents in the customer companies but from sincere discussions with the people in the trenches who deal with the company's product or service on a daily basis.

5. *Soliciting noncustomers (Effectiveness: 7)*. This most valuable source of information is seldom tapped. Asking customers why they have not considered a company's product or service may wake them up. Further, asking how satisfied they are with the various features and aspects of a competitor is a valuable source of information for improving the company's own performance.

6. *Soliciting former customers (Effectiveness: 9)*. The principal reason for soliciting customers who are leaving is to win them back. Success-

ful companies can recover at least 50% of such defecting customers. The follow-up with this defecting group is best done with a SWAT team that is staffed by some of the company's most customer-sensitive marketeers. Customers who leave provide a perspective on the business that is not always obvious from the inside. Further, what causes one customer to defect may be an early warning signal that others may follow—the rockslide could turn into an avalanche! Unlike conventional market research, feedback from defecting customers is concrete and specific. It does not attempt to measure attitudes or satisfaction, which are changeable and subjective. Defecting customers are usually able to articulate their reasons for leaving, and skillful probing can determine the root cause.

7. *Inputs from customer-contact personnel (Effectiveness: 8).* Customer-contact personnel inputs are important for identifying customer requirements (as mentioned in Chapter 8) and they are absolutely essential in assessing customer satisfaction. They are the frontline troops in the battle for the hearts and minds of customers. Jan Carlzon, the dynamic former chairman of SAS Airlines, in his seminal book *Moments of Truth* (Ballinger Publishing Company, 1987), calls the numerous contacts between customer-contact employees and their customers "fifty million moments of truth." It is these contacts—billing, telephone calls, reservations, complaints, and so on—that are integrated in a customer's mind and can make or break a company's reputation as a customer-caring organization. In fact, customers can, and often do, generalize about an entire organization based upon a single moment of truth! As far as customers are concerned, frontline employees *are* the company.

Unfortunately, myopic management seldom solicits the opinions, ideas, and suggestions of these frontline troops. As a result, when customers complain about a service, employees respond with a knee-jerk reaction: "Please write to the company. Management won't listen to us." Progressive companies regularly tap this vast reservoir of their employees' knowledge of customers' gripes, preferences, and suggestions for improvement. It is no wonder that in some of these progressive companies, the organizational pyramid is turned upside down: The customer is on top, the frontline employees next in rank, and the CEO at the bottom. The CEO is now a servant—not in a menial sense, but in a parental sense. The CEO serves employees and customers by coaching them, supporting them, and helping them grow and reach the maximum of their potential.

8. *One-on-one interviews (Effectiveness: 9)*. This is the most expensive and time-consuming approach, but also the most productive. It should always be used with core customers. Such customers deserve individual attention, with in-depth interviews, as described in Chapter 8. The people interviewed at the customer company should be those who make or influence the purchasing decisions as well as those who actually use the product or services. The interviewers should be members of the supplier company's senior management; an alternative is to use outside agencies or consultants, with whom customers are more likely to be completely straightforward. These one-on-one interviews should be frequent to keep the supplier company's finger constantly on the customer's pulse.

9. *Mass customization (Effectiveness: 10)*. This innovation, made possible by the explosion of information technology and flexible manufacturing systems, is fully described in Chapter 8. Most managers confuse variety with customization. Variety means the proliferation—or, rather, pollution—of options. As recently as a few years ago, U.S. car companies offered so many options that there could be more than 2,000 versions of each model, none of them exactly alike! Customization means manufacturing a product or delivering a service precisely in response to a particular customer's needs; mass customization means doing it in a cost-effective way. Mass customization calls for a customer-centered orientation in production and delivery processes—this requires a company to collaborate with individual customers in designing each one's requirements, which are then constructed from a base of pre-engineered modules that can be assembled in myriad ways.

Pine, Peppers, and Rogers cite the case of Ross Controls in Troy, Michigan, a manufacturer of valves and air-control systems ("Do You Want to Keep Your Customers Forever?", *Harvard Business Review*, March-April 1995). Ross learns about each customer's need and customizes the design of the product to meet that need. This involves spending time on the phone, faxing ideas back and forth, and visiting customer plants to see customer applications. Ross then makes prototypes and encourages its customers to suggest continuous upgrades. The designs are stored in a library of design platforms. Through the effective use of computer-aided design (CAD) and computer numerically controlled (CNC) machines, Ross electronically transmits tooling instructions from engineering work stations to high-speed production equipment, which can turn around new designs in as little as a day!

10. *Learning relationships (Effectiveness: 10).* Learning relationships are derived from mass customization. They provide the cement that holds customers and a company together—for life. In learning relationships, individual customers actually coach a company more and more about their preferences and needs, giving it a powerful competitive advantage. Again, consider Ross Controls as an example. The company has reinforced its learning relationships using its mass customization technique to the point where it commands the loyalty of such giant customers as General Motors, Knight Industries, Reynolds Aluminum, and Japan's Yamamura Glass. GM's Metal Fabrication Division will not go to any other company for its pneumatic valves and will not allow its suppliers to do so either. Knight Industries gives Ross 100% of its custom business. When a competitor tried to woo Knight away, Knight responded, "Why would I switch to you? You are *five product generations* behind where we are with Ross!"

Informal, Nonquantifiable Customer Feedback

There are other channels by which customers can give feedback to a company. Even though they are nonquantifiable, they can provide additional perspectives on customer satisfaction.

- *800 numbers*: Many companies have installed 800-number call-in lines that customers can use to seek answers to their questions or to complain. Such 800 lines are so productive that a few companies have their senior managers answer these lines once a month to receive direct customer feedback.
- *Listening at trade shows*: Comments of the viewing public at trade shows picked up by company representatives, or with hidden tape recorders, often provide useful pointers.
- *"Quickie cards"*: Many companies include a prepaid questionnaire card with their products that customers can fill out to indicate how well the product has worked for them. Such "zero-time" inputs can also give companies "infant mortality" reliability data. Incentives can be built in so that customers are encouraged to return the cards.

- *Customer/distributor/dealer councils*: It is always an excellent idea for a company to form councils with selected customers, distributors, and dealers to receive feedback. Distributors and dealers can greatly influence sales, negatively or positively, by their recommendations to prospective customers.

Customer Satisfaction Metrics

This section outlines the most prevalent metrics used to measure customer satisfaction. As in customer feedback methods, each metric is given an effectiveness scale from 1 to 10, with 1 being the least and 10 the most effective.

1. *Warranty costs (Effectiveness: 2)*. Most companies track their warranty costs, usually as a percentage of sales. This is a horrendous indication of customer dissatisfaction and it comes far too late. Further, it is just the tip of the iceberg: The company has no idea of the failures *after* the warranty period (which is usually only one year). These failures are much greater in number and more serious in terms of customer dissatisfaction than are the in-warranty failures. The customer feels he is being hung out to dry!

2. *Customer complaints/claims (Effectiveness: 5)*. This is an important statistic—but, as in the case of warranty costs, it comes too late. The damage is already done. Many companies, instead of correcting the problems, hide behind "No trouble found!" and use excuses like unconfirmed failure, customer misuse, customer's lack of knowledge in operating the product or service, and even (in a few cases) customer fraud to exonerate themselves. These excuses are sleeping pills. When the company wakes up, it may well be out of business. On the other hand, a complaining customer is much more useful to a company than one who simply and quietly switches suppliers. If the complaints are rectified speedily and completely, many customer defections can be prevented.

3. *Market share (Effectiveness: 2)*. Though popular as a measure of company performance, market share is not an accurate gauge of customer satisfaction and is even more nebulous as a gauge of customer loyalty. It measures the quantity, not the quality, of a company's ser-

vices to its customers. It does not distinguish between new customers and old customers, nor does it distinguish between one-time customers and lifetime customers. It compares the company only against its competitors. It does not determine whether the market as a whole is growing in importance or is fading. And there is the "sleeper effect," in which market share may be maintained for a few quarters but unexpectedly plunges because of cumulative customer dissatisfaction over time.

4. *Cost of poor quality (Effectiveness: 4).* This metric has been explained in detail in Chapter 7. It could be an excellent metric (and upgraded to an effectiveness of 8) if the cost of a defecting customer can be estimated, as outlined in that chapter. But 99% of companies do not even recognize this colossal loss, much less know how to estimate it.

5. *Industry reports (Effectiveness: 7).* This subject has been covered in Chapter 9. Of the many types of such reports, the ones issued by J. D. Powers are the fairest, most accurate, and most eagerly tracked by the affected companies.

6. *Business statistics.* In addition to the above measures, there are a number of ways in which customer satisfaction can be measured with business statistics:

- *Ratio of sales wins to sales losses (Effectiveness: 8).* This ratio should be calculated in several ways: by volume; by sales dollars; and over specific lengths of time.
- *Capture ratio (Effectiveness: 6).* This is the ratio of new customers to the number of proposals to win them.
- *Conversion efficiency (Effectiveness: 6).* Efficiency is measured by assessing the number of new customers per dollar of investment.
- *Mean time between winning a customer and losing that customer (Effectiveness: 6).*
- *Customer satisfaction index (Effectiveness: 7).* The CSI is found by using the equation

$$\frac{S}{I_1} - \frac{LS}{I_2}$$

where

S =   Sales from satisfied customers

I_1 =   Investment to ensure satisfied customers

LS   =   Lost sales from dissatisfied customers
I_2 =   Investment to save dissatisfied customers

For another approach to calculating CSI, see Chapter 11.

Business statistics have their advantages. They are quantified and can show trends over time. Management understands them, is sensitive to them, and can use them to initiate corrective action. The disadvantages of such statistics are the numerous variables affecting customer satisfaction or dissatisfaction that may be hard to pinpoint as root causes.

Customer Loyalty Metrics

Paradoxically, customer loyalty, though even more esoteric, is actually easier to measure than customer satisfaction. The polling and the voting is done with the customers' feet! There are several measures (each is given, as in customer satisfaction metrics, an effectiveness scale from 1 to 10):

1. *Maintenance ratio (Effectiveness: 8):* The ratio of the number of current customers retained to the number who have defected.

2. *Defection Rate (Effectiveness: 10):* The number of customers who have defected as a percentage of the total number of customers. Any figure over 10% should be cause for pushing the panic button! (Those customers that should be eliminated [see Chapter 2] are not included in this metric.)

3. *Amount and continuity of core customers (Effectiveness: 10):* An assessment done by number, by dollars, and by time.

4. *Longevity of core customers (Effectiveness: 10):* The total sales generated by long-term customers over several years is an excellent measure of customer loyalty.

5. *Value to core customer (Effectiveness: 10:)* The dollars saved to core customers in terms of quality, cost, cycle time, productivity, etc. (especially over time) is, or should be, the main objective of a company. Preferably, this metric should be developed in conjunction with the customer. It promotes mutual loyalty and mutual profit.

Step 5: Measuring Customer Satisfaction and Customer Loyalty	Rating				
	1	2	3	4	5
A. Quality Metrics					
1. The company systematically measures plant quality, with parameters such as outgoing quality; total defects per unit; yields/cycle time charts; and Cp and Cp$_k$ for individual product/ process characteristics.					
2. The company systematically measures field reliability, with parameters such as warranty costs, claims, and complaints.					
3. The company systematically gathers the cost of poor quality—including the cost and longevity of customer defections.					
4. The company systematically measures the cost of retrofits, recalls, product liability suits, and legal costs associated with the settlement of such suits.					
B. Industry and Independent Reports					
1. The company utilizes industry reports, such as J. D. Powers, and government and university sources to determine customer satisfaction compared with its competition.					
2. The company utilizes reports by magazines such as *Consumers Union* to determine an evaluation of the company's product or services compared with its competition.					
3. The company commissions independent laboratories to compare its products against those of its competition.					

Step 5: Measuring Customer Satisfaction and Customer Loyalty (cont'd)	Rating				
	1	2	3	4	5
C. Business Statistics					
The company uses several business statistics, such as ratio of sales wins to sales losses, customer satisfaction index, etc., to measure customer satisfaction.					
D. Direct Customer Surveys					
1. The company uses a survey instrument where the customer, rather than the company, selects the parameters of customer satisfaction to be measured.					
2. The parameters measured are those that are most important to the customer and the total number does not exceed 25.					
3. The survey instrument always includes the following questions: ▪ "Would you buy this product (or service) again?" ▪ "Would you buy a product of the same brand name?" ▪ "Would you recommend this product (or service) to a friend?" ▪ "How do you view similar products or services from our competitors?" ▪ "How can we better serve you?"					
4. The company de-emphasizes mail and telephone surveys and concentrates instead on one-on-one surveys of its core customers.					
5. The company solicits inputs on its products and services regularly from former customers and on competitors' products and services from non-customers.					

Step 5: Measuring Customer Satisfaction and Customer Loyalty (cont'd)	Rating				
	1	2	3	4	5
6. The company regularly taps the knowledge of its customer-contact employees in determining customer satisfaction.					
7. The company uses business statistics, such as the defection rate of customers, to measure customer loyalty.					
8. The company measures loyalty of its core customers by their number, by dollars, and by time.					
9. The company measures loyalty of its core customers by the value that core customers perceive they have received from the company.					
10. The company is moving toward mass customization and building learning relationships with its core customers.					

11

Step 6: Analyzing Customer, Former Customer, Noncustomer, and Competitor Feedback

"Minimal customer feedback analysis is corporate atrophy; excessive feedback analysis is corporate paralysis."

Keki R. Bhote

Potholes on the Road to Analysis

Research firms report that customer satisfaction research is the fastest growing area of their businesses, exceeding $100 million in revenues per year, according to a recent article in *Advertising Age* (Laura Lord, "Satisfaction Research Booms," February 10, 1992). However, much that can be gained from such customer satisfaction research is wasted, as companies oscillate between two extremes in analyzing feedback from customers—either they do little or no analysis, or they perform such microscopic analysis that effective corrective action gets lost in data churning. As David Futrell points out in "Ten Reasons Why Surveys Fail" (*Quality Progress*, April 1994), there are several pitfalls that should be avoided.

Ignoring Nonresponses

Mail surveys, in general, have poor response rates (5 to 10%). In general, people who respond either love or hate the product, so there is a sizable nonresponse population that can grossly skew the results.

Example: A county that had not allowed the sale of liquor since the days of Prohibition wanted to increase its tax revenues by lifting the ban. Concerned whether a measure to legalize liquor would pass, it polled a sample of 1,200 registered voters by mail. The response rate was low—only 25%. Of those who responded, 70% indicated opposition and the county abandoned the effort. However, the ballot passed by a 2:1 margin two years later. The original negative response was weighted by those strongly opposed to legalizing liquor, including church groups that were urged during religious services to return the surveys. The disproportionate results could have been corrected by contacting a few dozen nonrespondents by telephone.

Treating Customer Perceptions as Objective Measures

Sometimes, there is poor correlation between the numbers that indicate customer satisfaction—which is a perception—and those from more direct measures of performance, such as quality. Customer satisfaction is a complex phenomenon. It is influenced not only by product performance, but also by speed of corrective action, helpfulness of customer contact personnel, salespeople's effectiveness, and so on. It is worth a company's time to explore the link between customer satisfaction and other causative influences.

Example: A U.S. auto manufacturer compared results from customer satisfaction surveys that rated initial quality (first 90 days) to warranty records for the same cars for the same 90 days. But it was a weak correlation. The customers rated the cars as being much more reliable than the more objective warranty data showed. Further, there was a strong *negative* correlation between the customers' satisfaction with their dealers and the cars' actual failure rates. How do we explain the discrepancy? By making their customers happy, dealers were able to reduce the negative impact of the actual higher failure rates.

Treating Surveys as a One-Time Event, Not as an Ongoing Process

A one-time survey measures customer satisfaction at only one point in time. It cannot predict changes in customer satisfaction due to changes in product quality, customer expectations, or a competitor's advances. There should be periodic surveys and customer satisfaction levels should be plotted to observe trends over time.

Example: In a carpet manufacturer's customer satisfaction survey, customers rated the company as one of the top in the industry. Two years later, the company had lost almost half of its market share. The reason: The competition was selling carpets with stain-resistant protectants. The company had ignored this feature, deciding not to offer it because of added costs. But the customers saw it as a very important feature. Periodic surveys conducted at four-month intervals would have provided a warning so that the company could have reacted much earlier.

Asking Too General and Nonspecific Questions

Asking a broadly phrased question does not elicit details about the root cause of satisfaction or dissatisfaction.

Example: A car dealership asked customers who had their cars repaired by the service department, "How satisfied were you with our service department?" They were asked to circle one of the following: very dissatisfied, somewhat dissatisfied, somewhat satisfied, or very satisfied. "Dissatisfied" was the overwhelming response. But because of the time needed to administer and analyze the survey, the company lost valuable time. Too late, it realized that it should have asked more detailed questions. A good survey would have included questions about

- ease of making service appointments,
- courtesy of the service employees,
- professionalism of the service writer,
- price of repairs,
- repair time,
- convenience of hours, and
- loan car availability.

Failing to Ask Questions That Are Important to Customers

Related to asking too general questions is failing to ask the right questions, i.e., questions that are truly important to customers.

Example: A plastics manufacturer mailed a detailed questionnaire to a sample of 1,800 customers. The response was good (720 respondents). But many customers did not answer all of the multiple-choice or fixed-answer questions. However, the open-ended questions were filled out completely, with several additional pages of comments. This indicated that the questions were inappropriate and not about issues that were important to the customers.

Using Incorrect or Incomplete Analysis Methods

Most analyzers of survey data are unfamiliar with more sophisticated techniques to interpret such data. However, the use of design of experiments techniques like the multi-vari, paired comparisons, B vs. C (Tukey) tests, scatter plots, multiple regression, and multispecification search are powerful tools to analyze survey data.

Example: A mail order company that sells linens and down comforters was starting a new advertising campaign. Before launching the campaign, management wanted to determine which factors would provide the greatest customer appeal in the catalog advertisements showing down comforters. The factors included a wide array of concerns, related to both the advertising presentation and the product: sharp vs. soft camera focus; close vs. distant photo range; duck vs. goose down; pricing in a grid layout vs. pricing each item under its description; and catalogs wrapped in plastic vs. brown paper covers.

The company formulated a list of several outputs that would constitute advertising success: value; perceived quality; appearance; and intention to buy. Different factors were good for some outputs and not others. This required the use of more complex multiple regression and multi-specification search techniques, whereby one set of advertising factors clearly emerged as the best for simultaneously optimizing all of the survey measures.

Ignoring the Results

If the survey does not result in follow-up action, it is better not to survey in the first place. At best, such surveys are a waste of resources, and at worst they raise expectations in the minds of customers that cannot be fulfilled.

Example: A U.S. manufacturer relocated several hundred workers from an urban area in the North to a rural community in the South. The relocated workers started to complain about the local school system's poor quality. A survey of the parents yielded a high response rate and showed uniform criticism of the schools.

The company contacted the school system to offer support for improving the system, only to find that the school had no funds and no plans for improvement. The manufacturer had no power to change the school system and had acted irresponsibly, raising the expectations of the employees by conducting the survey in the first place.

Using Results Incorrectly

Some companies tie customer satisfaction ratings to a reward system. If the tie-in is direct (cause and effect), the reward makes sense. For example, flight attendants can and do directly affect passenger satisfaction. But accountants working for an automobile manufacturer have little impact on customer satisfaction.

Another misuse is to base rewards on surveys that are not precise enough to measure satisfaction.

Example: A telecommunications company decided to reward its employees with a bonus if it achieved a 1% improvement in customer satisfaction in a given month. But a control chart revealed that the inherent variation in customer satisfaction—with no improvements in the product being measured—was 5% from month to month. Employees were being rewarded for no actual improvement in customer satisfaction.

Developing a Single Customer Satisfaction Index and Comparisons with Competition

A prevalent practice in industry is to develop a single overall score—generally from 1 to 100—that integrates and quantifies various business parameters. The development of such a single score, one that can combine the many elements of customer satisfaction or enthusiasm (as listed in FIGURES 11 and 12), is similarly desirable to measure and analyze customer satisfaction for core customers.

One method is illustrated in FIGURE 19. It is a generic model for products. The first column lists the specific requirements the core cus-

FIGURE 19: Customer Satisfaction Index (CSI):
Generic Model for Products

Requirement	Importance (I) Scale: 1–5	Co. Rating (R) Scale: 1–5	Co. Score: (S) $(S) = (I) \times (R)$	Competitor Rating (CR) Scale: 1–5	Competitor Score (CS) $(CS) = (I) \times (CR)$
Quality (upon receipt)					
Reliability (within warranty)					
Durability (lifetime)					
Serviceability					
Up-time (% use)					
Tech. performance					
Features (that sell)					
Safety					
Human engineering					
Reputation					
Sales cooperativeness					
Price					
Resale price					
Delivery					
Total Score	Sum of (I) = (Y)		Sum of (S) = (T)		Sum of (CS) = U

Customer Satisfaction Index (CSI) expressed as a percentage:

a) For Co: $= \dfrac{T}{5Y} \times 100$

b) For competitor $= \dfrac{U}{5Y} \times 100$

tomers consider essential. These requirements can be derived from a QFD study or through one-on-one interviews. The list should not be too long or too short; generally, 10 to 15 parameters with top priorities as determined by the customer, not by the company, is the norm.

The second column depicts the importance (I) that customers attach to each requirement on a scale of 1 to 5, with 1 having the lowest importance and 5 the highest. In the third column, customers rate the company's performance (R) for each requirement, again on the same scale of 1 to 5. The fourth column multiplies the figures in columns 2 and 3 to determine the company's score for each requirement: (S) = (I) x (R).

To determine the overall customer satisfaction index (CSI), the importance numbers in column 2 are totaled (Y), as are the scores in column 4 (T); the overall index for customer satisfaction is expressed as a percentage: T/5Y x 100. (By multiplying the sum of the importance numbers [Y] with the maximum rating a company can receive [5], a maximum possible score [5Y] is achieved against which the actual performance score [T] can be compared. Maximum CSI is 100%.) A CSI for a company of 50% or less would signal a looming crisis. A CSI of 80% or higher would be a sign of robust customer health.

The same CSI can be expanded to determine how the customer assesses a company's best competitor. The fifth column is the customer's rating of the competitor's performance (CR) for each requirement, also on a scale of 1 to 5. The sixth column multiples the numbers in columns 2 and 5 to determine a competitor's score for each requirement: (CS) = (I) x (CR).

To determine an overall CSI for the competitor, the scores in column 6 (CS) are totaled (U). The overall CSI for the competitor, then, is U/5Y x 100, also expressed as a percentage.

FIGURE 20 illustrates the use of a CSI where a large original equipment manufacturer rated its supplier, which provided engineers to this company on a contract basis. It also rated a competitive supplier. While the overall CSIs were close for the two supplier companies, there were considerable differences between the two in the ratings for the individual requirements. For example, the company is superior to its competitor in two requirements that are very important to the customer: placement speed and placement professionalism. But the company's high cost for services needs to be reduced. It also needs to enhance its reputation in the eyes of its customer.

FIGURE 20: Customer Satisfaction Index (CSI) of a Company Providing Engineering Services on Contract (Rated by the Original Equipment Manufacturer Company Contracting for the Service)

Requirement	Importance (I) Scale: 1–5	Co. Rating (R) Scale: 1–5	Co. Score: (C) $(S) = (I) \times (R)$	Competitor Rating (CR) Scale: 1–5	Competitor Score (CS) $(CS) = (I) \times (CR)$
Placement Speed	4	5	20	3	12
Placement professionalism	5	4	20	2	10
Low cost	4	2	8	5	20
Dependability	3	4	12	3	9
Flexibility	1	3	3	5	5
Cooperativeness	2	4	8	3	6
Reputation	3	4	12	5	15
	Tot (Y) = 22		Tot (T) = 83		Tot (U) = 77

Co.: CSI: $\dfrac{T}{5Y} \times 100 = \dfrac{83}{110} \times 100 = 75\%$

Competitor: CSI: $\dfrac{U}{5Y} \times 100 = \dfrac{77}{110} = 70\%$

The same CSI can be used for internal customers. FIGURE 21 depicts how the sponsor of a training project rated an internal supplier team that designed the training manual. The overall CSI was a poor 53%. The team also received low scores for several individual requirements that the internal customer deemed important.

The elegance of the customer satisfaction index is the remarkable way in which it simultaneously analyzes

- the relative importance customers attach to their priority requirements;
- the strengths and weaknesses of the company regarding those requirements, as determined by the customer; and
- the strengths and weaknesses of the company as compared with its best competition, again as determined by the customer.

FIGURE 21: Internal Customer Satisfaction Index (CSI) of a Team
Designing a Training Manual
(Rated by the Project Sponsor)

Requirement	Importance (I) Scale: 1–10	Rating (R) Scale: 1–5	Score (S) S = (I) × (R)
1. *Quality*			
• Completeness	7	4	28
• Accuracy	9	1	9
• Clarity	8	3	24
• Meaningfulness	10	2	20
2. *Timeliness*			
• On-time delivery	8	1	8
• Cycle time	5	1	5
3. *Cost (to customer)*	6	3	18
4. *Dependability*			
• Promises kept	4	2	8
• Credibility	6	3	18
• Trustworthiness	7	2	14
5. *Cooperativeness*			
• Responsiveness	5	4	20
• Flexibility	4	3	12
• Approachability	6	5	30
• Courtesy	4	5	20
6. *Communication*			
• Listening	4	4	16
• Feed forward information	5	2	10
Total Score	Total (Y) = 98		Total (T) = 260

Customer Satisfaction Index (CSI) $= \dfrac{T}{5Y} \times 100 = \dfrac{260}{490} \times 100 = 53\%$

Step 6: Analyzing Customer, Former Customer, Non-customer, and Competitor Feedback	Rating				
	1	2	3	4	5
A. Survey Instrument Design					
1. The company continually reassesses its survey instruments, such as its questionnaires, to make sure that they are adequate, relevant, and customer-sensitive.					
2. The company realizes that a change in survey instrument format (and the baseline of questions) is necessary in tracking customer satisfaction progress if the marketplace has changed.					
3. The company uses surveys as a continuous process, not a one-time event.					
B. Feedback Data Analysis					
1. The company follows up with customers who did not respond to surveys.					
2. The company uses only the "very satisfied" or "excellent" ratings, as opposed to merely "satisfied," in determining customer loyalty.					
3. The company uses an overall customer satisfaction index (CSI) to determine its strengths and weaknesses relative to its customers' important requirements.					
4. The company uses an overall CSI to determine its strengths and weaknesses relative to its best competitors.					
C. Former Customers. The company regularly analyzes the reasons for its customer defections and mounts a massive effort to win defecting customers back (see Chapter 12).					

Step 6: Analyzing Customer, Former Customer, Non-customer, and Competitor Feedback (cont'd)	Rating				
	1	2	3	4	5
D. Noncustomers. The company regularly assesses the reasons why noncustomers stay away from the company's products or services, and it institutes remedial actions.					
E. Information Technology. The company utilizes information technology to obtain a complete profile of each core customer and attempts to provide preferential services to such customers.					
F. Dropping Customers. The company identifies those customers that need to be terminated in order to concentrate on preferred and core customers and enhance its own profitability.					

12

Step 7: Continuous Improvement

"Customer loyalty is a journey, not a destination."

John J. Creedon, CEO, Met Life

Customer Loyalty—No Finish Line

After the management team finishes analyzing customer and competitive feedback, the hard task of correcting the causes of customer complaints and customer dissatisfaction begins. Remember that even if customers are satisfied, there is no guarantee that they will be repeat customers. Their requirements need continued assessment. Further, no effort should be spared in ongoing initiatives to *earn* loyalty and faithfulness. In short, attaining and maintaining customer satisfaction—especially customer *loyalty*—is a journey without end. It is said frequently about quality, "There is no finish line." There is no finish line for customer loyalty, either.

This chapter concentrates on several facets of a continuous improvement process, starting with complaints and problems perceived by customers and the measures needed to correct them.

Typical Customer Complaints, Their Causes, and Remedial Techniques

Although there may be a myriad of customer complaints, they can be divided into a few broad categories. TABLE 4 lists the most typical

TABLE 4: Typical Customer-Reported Problems, Their Causes, and Corrective Tools

Area	Causes	Appropriate corrective tools
Poor product quality	▪ Poor design	▪ Design of experiments (DOE)
	▪ Poor manufacturing	▪ Design of experiments; total productive maintenance (TPM)
	▪ Poor material from suppliers	▪ Design of experiments
	▪ Poor workmanship	▪ Poka-yoke
Poor product reliability	Designs not robust with time and field stresses	Multiple environment overstress testing (MEOST) and DOE
Product liability potential	▪ Poor design for human and product safety	▪ Product liability prevention (PLP)
	▪ Customer misapplication	▪ Misapplication proof design; warning label
Poor field repair service	▪ Unmotivated repairmen	▪ Job redesign; reengineering the repair process
	▪ Poor training, tools	▪ Built-in diagnostics
	▪ Parts nonavailability	▪ Reliability improvement, reducing necessity for spare parts
Customer misuse	Instruction not read or followed	Warranty labels; fail-safe designs
Customer noncomprehension	Nonuser-friendly features	Ergonomics, training

Area	Causes	Appropriate corrective tools
Late delivery	Poor forecasts; master schedules; MRPII; equipment breakdowns; supplier delinquency	Pull systems; Just-in-Time (JIT); total productive maintenance (TPM); small lots; reduced set-up times; supply management
Disconnected distributors/dealers	Limited loyalty to company	Distribution/dealer/customer councils
Order processing, billing, accounts receivables errors	Order inaccuracies, backorders, poor order tracking, routing errors, returns processing	Flowcharting; next operation as customer; business process re-engineering
Customer-contact employees not empowered	▪ Untrained, unmotivated, underpaid employees ▪ Company rules and regulations as a straightjacket ▪ Financial adjustments to customers unheard of	▪ Customer sensitivity training, "moments of truth" principles reinforced; more management attention (Hawthorne effect); pay incentives ▪ De-emphasize all rules that do not or adversely affect the customer ▪ Authorize employees (up to certain limits) to compensate angry, dissatisfied customers
Dictatorial management	Management by fear; micromanagement	Management must change to leadership. Only the board of directors can effect the transition.

problem areas, their causes, and the most appropriate tools and techniques to correct them. Strange as it may seem, many of those techniques are not even known to most companies, much less used by them!

As an example, a *Fortune* 500 company launched a drive for a 10:1 improvement for its field reliability. The objective was right on target, but the results were not. Halfway through this five-year goal, the company was one-and-a-half years behind in its timetable and losing ground each month. The corrective actions were reminiscent of practices 20 years ago. Pareto prioritization, cause-and-effect diagrams, committees, finger-pointing, and responsibility transference to some other group (such as suppliers or designers) were the poor tools being used. With a sense of urgency, the company switched to powerful tools like multiple environment overstress tests and the design of experiments to solve these chronic field problems. It is now well on its way to beating by a full year its original goal of a 10:1 improvement in five years.

Management Audits

Companies use management audits to monitor and improve the effectiveness of services rendered to customers, especially in the service sector. These audits may be announced or unannounced. Airline executives put themselves in the customers' shoes, starting with phoning for a reservation and monitoring the entire experience of waiting in line for a ticket; they assess gate procedures, flight service, courtesy, and baggage handling. Hotel executives, likewise, simulate a customer's encounters with the hotel, from the parking lot and the reception desk to the cashier and check-out procedure. The chairman of the board of the renowned Marriott chain periodically becomes a bellhop to learn, firsthand, about the service a hotel offers!

From 800 Numbers to Ombudsman to Chief Customer Officer (CCO)

Many companies facilitate their link with customers through the use of 800 numbers—a channel for customers to voice inquiries, concerns, and complaints. To demonstrate their commitment to customers, senior managers in a few enterprising companies answer these 800 number phone lines one day a month. They receive unfiltered feedback directly from customers by this method, instead of regurgitated data fed to them by subordinates.

Some companies go further and appoint a senior executive as ombudsman to provide a master information center for customers who might otherwise get lost in a corporate maze. The ultimate achievement in this direction is the appointment of a top management person as the company's chief customer officer (CCO) to be the customer's advocate in the entire corporation and to act as its "customer conscience."

"Statistics and Damned Statistics!"

It is said that "Figures do not lie, but liars figure. They use statistics!" There are good means of using statistics and bad. Many companies, enamored of number crunching, use it indiscriminately. Employing the seven tools of quality control, widely practiced by the Japanese, is an example of using poor statistical tools for the wrong application. These tools, including plan-do-study-act (PDSA), Pareto charts, cause and effect diagrams, frequency distributions, and control charts, are elementary and inadequate for problem solving in production. They are even worse used in evaluating business practices or in dealing with customers.

Design of experiments (DOE) techniques, on the other hand, are powerful tools for preventing and solving product and process problems; more and more, they are being used for analyzing and improving customer performance. Some of these techniques are briefly described here.

Multivari Study

The purpose of the multivari technique is not necessarily to find the root cause of a problem (the No. 1 cause is called the Red X), but to subdivide the various causes into families (where the Red X may be located) and filter out those families that may not contain the root cause—in other words, it is a process of elimination.

Example: A major telephone company was faced with mounting customer complaints and a potential loss of sales. The complex telephone system customer feedback had been divided into:

1. The number of troubles reported.
2. The duration of each trouble.

But there was no further stratification of the data. A multivari study was undertaken to break down the families of trouble by:

1. Class of service.
2. Trouble code: exchange access, no trouble found (NTF), and other.
3. Time: week, day, shift, and hour.
4. Customer type.
5. Service center.
6. Geographic location.
7. Operator.

The stratification revealed that there were no significant differences in the quantity or duration of the interruptions among six of the seven families (stratifications). However, the NTF in the trouble code (second family) was the dominant cause, or Red X. This pinpointed cause led to an investigation of the reason for the intermittency in the electronic equipment. Useless fingerpointing stopped; the multivari study "talked to the process" and solved the problem.

Paired Comparisons

Paired comparisons is another simple but powerful technique that compares good and bad units (generally, in pairs) and examines a number of parameters, or quality characteristics, in each pair. Repetition of differences in a particular parameter in each pair gives a clue to the Red X.

Applied to customer satisfaction, paired comparisons identify six to eight "good" customers—preferably the best-of-the-best (BOB)—and six to eight "bad" customers—preferably the worst-of-the-worst (WOW), in terms of complaints. Various product and/or customer characteristics are then compared to see which show a repetitive difference.

Example: A large company was concerned about the loss of sales to its tough competitor. It felt that the root cause was a cost-cutting move it had instituted: The account executives who had been supported with a technical consultant on a one-on-one basis were each forced to share that technical consultant's services with three other account executives.

A paired comparison was made of sales wins vs. sales losses. The following characteristics were examined for repetitive differences:

1. Customer demographics—size, type, and location.
2. Time.
3. Product type and complexity.
4. Nature of the complaints.
5. Salespersons.
6. Sales support (one technical consultant per account executive vs. one consultant per four account executives).
7. Sales branch serving the customer.
8. Sales manager.
9. Amount of time spent with the customer.

It turned out that the ratio of technical consultants to account executives (number 6, above) was not the repetitive difference. In fact, management's decision to reduce that element of cost was the right one. The Red X was the amount of time spent by the salespeople with the customer.

B vs. C: Alpha (α) Risk

B vs. C is a powerful, yet economical, DOE technique to determine which of two items (processes, products, features, etc.) is better. "B" stands for the supposedly better method; "C" stands for the current method.

In product work, B vs. C is used to validate or to verify which of two products, processes, or methods is better, using very small sample sizes—usually three Bs and three Cs—and ranking the results (the output) in descending order of preference. Only if the three Bs are on top and the three Cs are at the bottom can it be said, with 95% confidence or 5% risk (α), that the B method is better than C.

In work with customers and markets, B vs. C is an equally economic and versatile tool. It can be used to compare:

- two models (say, in focus groups);
- two sales approaches;
- two test markets;
- two advertising campaigns;
- two product features;
- two cluster features (in conjoint analysis); or
- two suppliers (your company versus the competition).

Example: For two "clay model" design styles of a new product, a company invited three typical customers to a clinic and asked them to express their preferences for either design B or design C style. Three scenarios are possible:

Case 1:   All three customers preferred design C style.
Case 2:   Two of three customers preferred one design style over the other.
Case 3:   All three customers preferred design B style.

In Case 1, design C would most likely be the choice of the population at large. In Case 2, there is no clear signal on the preferred styles. The lowest cost design would, then, be used. In Case 3, design B would be the preferred style of the population.

B vs. C Beta (β) Risk

Sometimes, it is desirable to know whether the difference between the averages of two sets of data is statistically significant—say, between three Bs and three Cs.

If $\bar{X}B$ and $\bar{X}C$ are the B and C averages, respectively, the distance, $\bar{X}_B - \bar{X}_C$, should be a minimum of 2.7 σ_c (where σ_c is the standard deviation of the C data). This gives a Beta (β) risk of 10%, or a confidence of 90%.

Tukey Test

For a larger sample, the Tukey test ranks all observations B and C. The top end count, with all Bs only, and the other endcount, with all Cs only, are added up. The area of overlap where there are both Bs and Cs can be ignored. The total end count and the confidence levels of a significant difference are:

Total End Count	Confidence
6	90%
7	95%
10	99%
13	99.9%

The Tukey test is independent of sample size.

Scatter Plots

The use of scatter plots is another DOE technique to graphically portray the relationship between two variables—say, an output or dependent variable *versus* an input or independent variable. The tighter the scatter plot (parallelogram), the greater is the correlation between these variables.

Example: Scatter plots were drawn to determine the overall level of customer satisfaction of airline passengers with (1) on-time arrivals, and (2) meal service, as shown in FIGURE 22. The scatter plots indicate that customer satisfaction has no correlation with the quality of meal service. By contrast, there is a direct correlation between late arrival

FIGURE 22: Scatter Plots of Customer Satisfaction vs. Airline Time of Arrival and Quality of Meal Service

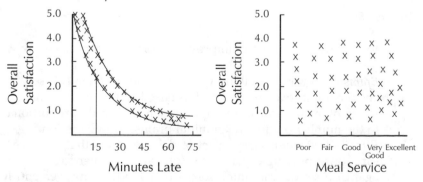

and customer satisfaction, which decreases rapidly if the plane is late by more than 10 minutes.

Multiple Regression Analysis

Scatter plots are generally useful if there are only two variables—a dependent output and an independent input. Often, however, there could be several (multiple) causes affecting a given output. Then a more rigorous mathematical model, such as multiple regression analysis, is needed to show the relationship between these variables.

Example: An airline wanted to determine which of several independent variables would cause a person to choose that airline repeatedly. The result of an extensive multiple regression analysis indicated the following:

Variable	Cumulative Adjusted R-Square
• Frequent-flier program	0.43
• Convenience of flight times	0.62
• On-time arrival	0.75
• Service on-board	0.82
• Baggage handling time	0.85

This indicated that 62% of the cumulative variance in a passenger's selection of that airline was based, primarily, on the attractiveness of its frequent flier program and secondarily on the convenience (multiple choices) of its flight times.

Creative Stimuli

Other tools can also be used to improve customer performance.

- *Brainstorming* is a well-known technique, frequently used by customer improvement teams. It is based on the premise that the worth of the final ideas for improvement is directly proportional to the number of ideas in an initial brainstorming session.
- *Force Field Analysis* arrays a set of driving forces that are necessary for improving a parameter (of, say, customer satisfaction) against a set of restraining forces that hinder improvement. It

then systematically plans measures to enhance the driving forces and simultaneously attenuate the restraining forces to achieve a much improved level of performance.

- *Value Engineering* is a powerful discipline that improves the quality of a product, service, or business process while simultaneously reducing its cost. Applied to any process or service that affects customers, it asks:

  - What does it do? (*what is the function of the process*)
  - What does it cost?
  - What else can perform the function? (*with improved performance*)
  - What will that cost? (*at lower cost*)

The improved process, generally, is a radical departure from the current one. Another facet of value engineering is asking the 5 *Why's*. Say we start with a question such as "Why do we need this process or method?" If the answer is "because of . . . such and such a factor," then ask a second "why"—i.e., "Why do we need this factor?" To that answer, you ask the third "why," and so on until the process is either eliminated altogether, minimized, or modified for greater customer acceptance and lower cost.

The "5 Why's" technique is especially useful in challenging those company activities that are not important to the customer and do not add real value.

Business Process Reengineering (BPR)

The ultimate application of business process reengineering (BPR) is to revolutionize the entire company—its organizational structure; its methods of hiring, evaluating, compensating, and promoting its employees; its very values and culture. Among the several companies that profess to have adopted BPR, hardly any have gone the full distance.

Nevertheless, there are a few BPR techniques that companies can adopt through evolution rather than its full-blown revolution:

- *Cross-Functional Teams* can be used to convert a bureaucratic, vertical organization into a hard-hitting horizontal, interdisciplinary team that can improve business processes and focus on customers.

- *Flowcharting.* The cross-functional teams use flowcharting (otherwise known as process mapping) to map every step in the business process, starting with the customer and going back to the start of the process. The cycle time (actual clock time) of each step as well as the total cycle time of the entire process are determined. Each step is then examined to see if it really adds value, especially from the customer's viewpoint. All non-value-added steps and their cycle times are then eliminated or drastically reduced. Typically, flowcharting can eliminate over two-thirds of the steps in such a process and half the total cycle time. The result is faster, higher-quality, and lower-cost service to the customer.
- *"Out-of-Box" Thinking.* Flowcharting is evolutionary—a starting point for improved service to the customer. It establishes only a base-camp in the climb to the top of the mountain. To get to the peak of maximum effectiveness, the entire process—flowchart and all—must be jettisoned using "out-of-box" thinking. This means developing radically new and creative ways to achieve process goals.

Customer-Contact Employees: Caring and Feeding

Japanese CEOs frequently state that their primary task is "the caring and feeding of their young," i.e., their newer employees. In the service sector, where employees come into frequent contact with customers, the top management of such companies must also "feed" and nurture such employees. In the reverse pyramid organizational structure that is gaining currency, customer-contact employees are at the top of the pyramid——next only to the external customers. They must be empowered, using the following measures:

- *Selection and hiring* should be based on sensitivity to customers and on team-player and innovative potential. They should not be picked off the streets and hired as a "pair of hands."
- *Compensation* should be commensurate with the importance of interface with customers.
- *Training* can never be overemphasized. It should deal not only with a thorough knowledge of products and services, but also

with skills in listening, innovation, and in ways to defuse customer frustrations and anger.

- *Decision making* should include the ability to change rules and regulations from those that serve the company to those that serve customers to capture their satisfaction and loyalty.
- *Morale* should constantly be assessed through management and customer surveys.
- *Recognition* by management for outstanding service to customers should become a way of life. It should include bonuses and other rewards, along with celebrations for the entire team.

Defections Management

Minimizing customer defections should be elevated to one of the most important tasks of a company. It starts with defection prevention, which is infinitely better than defection cure. The elements of prevention include:

- The establishment of a top-level customer steering committee.
- The elevation of a dynamic top manager to the post of chief customer officer (CCO), ranking above a COO or CFO.
- The creation of a customer-defection SWAT team, made up of the company's best marketeers and problem solvers.
- A mission statement that emphasizes the importance of lifelong customer retention. As an example, Mastercare, the auto-service subsidiary of Bridgestone/Firestone, states: "Our company's goal is to provide the service-buying public with a superior buying experience that will encourage them to return willingly and to share their experience with others." (See Reichheld and Sasser, "Zero Defections: Quality Comes to Services," *Harvard Business Review*, September-October 1990.)
- The establishment of defection rates as a key metric to improve value, as perceived by customers.
- An unequivocal commitment to be interested in the (core) customers long after a sale is consummated; to build learning relationships with them; and to constantly assess their changing needs and expectations.
- Tying incentives to defection rates as a key performance mea-

sure for senior management. Great West Life Assurance Company of Englewood, Colorado pays a 50% premium to group health insurance brokers who hit customer retention targets.

However, we don't live in a perfect world. Assuming that some customer defections are inevitable, what actions can be taken to minimize them?

- Identify those customers that are not worth keeping—the "dog" or "tin" customers described in Chapter 2—and encourage them to leave, with price increases or other disincentives. Such customer terminations should be excluded from defection measurements.
- Anticipate potential defections. A sharp decrease in sales or unit volumes should be a red flag. The customer SWAT team should pursue the reasons for such drops.
- Profile the percentage of time spent by senior managers on customer care vs. other activities (see TABLE 2).
- Have senior managers periodically answer 800 number calls to learn of customer problems firsthand.
- Monitor product quality and reliability as early as possible. Warranty and claims data are too late. Examine zero-time defects—i.e., as customers first experience the product. Examine the company's own outgoing quality audits. Analyze in-process reliability-oriented failures as early indicators of future product failures in the customer's hands.
- Establish key service stations as listening posts for customer problems and for comparisons with competition's products.
- Listen, listen, listen to your customer-contact employees, who come into frequent contact with customers; and *act, act, act* on their observations and ideas for improvement.
- Test the product or service to assure that it is user-friendly, easy to follow instructions, to install, to operate, to store, to service (preferably with built-in diagnostics).
- With the use of Information Technology (IT) and flexible manufacturing systems (FMS), develop a mass customization strategy that can customize each core customer's requirements and deliver the product or service at low cost and high speed.

Step 7: Continuous Improvement	Rating				
	1	2	3	4	5
A. Corrective Actions on Typical Customer Complaints					
1. The causes of the following typical customer complaints are identified and the appropriate corrective action tools utilized: *(a) product quality, (b) product reliability, (c) product liability, (d) field repair, (e) customer misuse, (f) customer noncomprehension, (g) delivery, (h) distributors/dealers, (i) customer services, (j) customer-contact employees, (k) management.*					
2. Top management regularly conducts audits of services rendered to customers.					
3. 1–800 numbers are made available to customers for contact with company officials.					
4. The company appoints an ombudsman, or preferably a Chief Customer Officer (CCO), to act as the customers' advocate within the company.					
5. The company utilizes design of experiments to analyze and improve customer performance.					
6. The company utilizes creative tools such as force field analysis and value engineering to improve customer performance.					
7. The customer utilizes business process improvement, flowcharting, and "out-of-box" thinking to improve service to customers.					
8. The company empowers its customer-contact employees to better service its customers.					
9. The company adopts defections management mission, goal, objectives, and detailed plans to prevent customer defections and attempt to keep customers for life.					

Conclusion

This briefing has advocated the case for a company to go beyond mere customer satisfaction to customer loyalty; to go beyond just market share, which is only quantity of performance, to customer retention, which is quality of performance; to go beyond today's customers to having customers for life. It has presented a roadmap for achieving customer loyalty. And it has lit the way with a self-assessment that a company can employ to determine how far it has traveled on the road to customer loyalty and how much farther it has to journey.

The results of long-term commitment to customer loyalty are captured in TABLE 5 (on next page).

The bottom line? Customer loyalty pays and pays handsomely.

Keki R. Bhote

Lessons Learned from This Briefing

1. 15% to 40% of customers who say they are satisfied **defect** from a company each year.
2. Although many companies are convinced that maximizing customer satisfaction maximizes profitability and market share, *fewer than 2% are able to measure bottom-line improvements* resulting from documented increases in levels of customer satisfaction.
3. **Totally** satisfied customers are *six times* more likely to repurchase a company's products over a span of one to two years than merely satisfied customers.
4. *A 5% reduction* in *customer defection* can result in profit increase from 30% to 85%.
5. **Loyal** customers provide higher profits, more repeat business, higher market share, and more referrals.
6. If companies increase their *customer retention* by 2%, it is the equivalent of cutting their operating costs by 10%.
7. It costs five to seven times more to find new customers than to *retain customers* you already have.
8. *One lifetime customer* is worth *$2 million* to a car company; *$1.5 million* to an airline.
9. *One loyal customer* can provide *$26,000* of revenue to an orange juice company by *word-of-mouth* advertising.
10. We need *new paradigms*: a shift from zero defects to *zero defections*, a shift from mass marketing to *mass customization*.

TABLE 5: The Return on Investment in Customer Loyalty

Parameter	Customer focused companies	Average company
Return on equity	17%	11%
Profit on sales	9.2%	5%
Market share growth	6%	2%
Cost reduction	10–15%	2–3%
Stock price growth	16.9%	10.9%

(K. Bhote, *Quality for Profit,* Strategic Directions Publishers, 1995)

Works Cited

Akao, Yoji: *Quality Function Deployment*, Productivity Press, 1988.

Bhote, Keki R.: *Next Operation As Customer*, American Management Association Briefing, 1991.

Bhote, Keki R.: *Quality for Profit*, Strategic Directions Publishers, 1995.

Bhote, Keki R.: *Strategic Supply Management*, American Management Association, 1989.

Bhote, Keki R.: *World Class Quality—Using Design of Experiments to Make It Happen*, American Management Association, 1991.

Boothroyd, Jeffrey and Peter Dewhurst: *Product Design for Manufacturing and Assembly*, Boothroyd & Dewhurst, Inc., 1987.

Cannie, J.K. and D. Chapman: *Keep Customers for Life*, American Management Association, 1991.

Carlzon, Jan: *Moments of Truth*, Ballinger Publishing Company, 1987.

Daviss, Bennett: "Revival of the Fittest," *Ambassador*, December, 1995.

Futrell, David: "Ten Reasons Why Surveys Fail," *Quality Progress*, April 1994.

Galvin, Robert W.: *Idea of Ideas*, Motorola University Press, 1991.

Icabucci, Dawn, Kent Grayson, and Amy Ostrom: "Customer Satisfaction Fables," *Sloan Management Review*, Summer 1994.

Jones, Thomas O. and W. Earl Sasser, Jr: "Why Satisfied Customers Defect," *Harvard Business Review*, November–December 1995.

Kearney, A.T.: *The Customer Satisfaction Audit*, Strategic Directions Publishers, Ltd., Zurich, Switzerland, 1994.

Lord, Laura: "Satisfaction Research Booms," *Advertising Age*, February 10, 1992.

Maguire, Brian: "Twelve Steps to Walking the Talk," *National Productivity Review*, Autumn 1995.

Miles, Larry : *Value Analysis Techniques*, McGraw-Hill, 1982.

Nakajima, Seiichi: *Total Productive Maintenance*, Productivity Press, 1988.

Peters, Thomas J. and Robert H. Waterman: *In Search of Excellence*, Harper & Row, 1982.

Pine, B. Joseph II, Don Peppers and Martha Rogers: "Do You Want to Keep Your Customers Forever?" *Harvard Business Review*, March–April 1995.

Reichheld, Frederick F. and W. Earl Sasser, Jr.: "Zero Defections: Quality Comes to Services," *Harvard Business Review*, September–October 1990.

REL Consultancy Group: "1994 Survey of Customer Retention and Corporate Profitability."

Shingo, Shigeo: *Zero Q. C. Source Inspection and Poka Yoke,* Productivity Press, 1985.

Spendolini, Michael: *The Benchmarking Book,* American Management Association, 1992.

Sprechler, Jay: *When America Does It Right,* Independent Engineering Management Practices, 1988.

About the Author

Keki R. Bhote is the President of Keki R. Bhote Associates, a company specializing in Quality and Productivity Improvement. He has consulted with over 300 companies globally ranging from diverse manufacturing and service industries to universities and governments.

Mr. Bhote has retired from Motorola, where he was Senior Corporate consultant on Quality and Productivity Improvement. He played a key role in Motorola winning the prestigious *Malcolm Baldrige National Quality Award*-and in launching its renowned *Six Sigma* process for continuous quality improvement. He is still a Consultant Emeritus with Motorola.

Mr. Bhote received a B.S. in Telecommunications Engineering from the University of Madras and his M.S. in Applied Physics and Engineering Sciences from Harvard University. He joined Motorola as a development engineer and rose through the ranks to become Group Director of Quality and Value Assurance for Motorola's Automotive and Industrial Electronics Group, before promotion to Senior Consultant for the whole corporation.

He is the author of nine books including *World Class Quality, Strategic Supply Management* and *Next Operation as Customer—How to Improve Quality, Cost and Cycle Time in Service Operations.*

OTHER AMA PUBLICATIONS OF INTEREST

PERIODICALS ORDER FORM

(Discounts for bulk orders of five or more copies.)

Please send me the following:

☐ ____ copies of **Beyond Customer Satisfaction to Customer Loyalty: The Key to Greater Profitability,** Stock #02362XFMC, $19.95/$17.95 AMA Members.

☐ ____ copies of **Blueprints for Innovation: How Creative Processes Can Make You and Your Company More Competitive,** Stock #02359XFMC, $14.95/$13.45 AMA Members.

☐ ____ copies of **Blueprints for Service Quality: The Federal Express Approach, SECOND EDITION,** Stock #02356XFMC, $12.50/$11.25 AMA Members.

☐ ____ copies of **Quality Alone Is Not Enough,** Stock #02349XFMC, $12.95/$11.65 AMA Members.

☐ ____ copies of **The Management Compass: Steering the Corporation Using Hoshin Planning,** Stock #02358XFMC, $19.95/$17.95 AMA Members.

Name: _____

Title: _____

Organization: _____

Street Address: _____

City, State, Zip: _____

Phone: ( ) _____

Sales tax, if applicable, and shipping & handling will be added.

☐ Charge my credit card   ☐ Bill me   ☐ AMA Member

Card #: _ _ _ _ _ _ _ _ _ _ _ _ _ _ _ _ Exp. Date _____

Signature: _____

Purchase Order #: _____

AMA'S NO-RISK GUARANTEE: If for any reason you are not satisfied, we will credit the purchase price toward another product or refund your money. **No hassles. No loopholes. Just excellent service. That is what AMA is all about.**

AMA Publication Services
P.O. Box 319
Saranac Lake, NY 12983